A Witch's
10 Commandments
*Magickal Guidelines
for Everyday Life*

Marian Singer

PROVENANCE
PRESS

Adams Media
Avon, Massachusetts

Provenance Press® is a registered trademark of F+W Publications, Inc.
Provenance Press® is an imprint of Adams Media
57 Littlefield Street
Avon, MA 02322
www.adamsmedia.com

ISBN 13: 978-1-59337-504-1
ISBN 10: 1-59337-504-2
Printed in Canada.
J I H G F E D C

Library of Congress Cataloging-in-Publication Data
Singer, Marian.
A witch's 10 commandments / Marian Singer.
p. cm.
  ISBN 1-59337-504-2
1. Witchcraft. 2. Magic. I. Title: Witch's ten commandments.
II. Title.
BF1566.S515 2006
299'.94--dc22
2006005105

This publication is designed to provide accurate and authoritative information with regard to the subject matter covered. It is sold with the understanding that the publisher is not engaged in rendering legal, accounting, or other professional advice. If legal advice or other expert assistance is required, the services of a competent professional person should be sought.

—From a *Declaration of Principles* jointly adopted by a
Committee of the American Bar Association and
a Committee of Publishers and Associations

Many of the designations used by manufacturers and sellers to distinguish their product are claimed as trademarks. Where those designations appear in this book and Adams Media was aware of a trademark claim, the designations have been printed with initial capital letters.

This book is available at quantity discounts for bulk purchases.
For information, please call 1-800-289-0963.

Judeo-Christian Ten Commandments taken from *The Holy Bible: King James Version*

Interior illustrations © Dover Publications.

Contents

Acknowledgments

I would like to take this opportunity to thank Ashleen, Mino, Daven, Cinnamon Moon, Bic, Alicia, Don & Dee, Dorothy, Bev, Danielle, Renee, Chuck, and the many other people who took time to speak to me from their hearts on this very complicated topic. Without your insights, counsel, and periodic reality checks, this book could not have been written.

The Judeo-Christian Ten Commandments

I. I am the Lord thy God, which have brought thee out
of the land of Egypt, out of the house of bondage. Thou shalt
have no other gods before me.

II. Thou shalt not make unto thee any graven image,
or any likeness of any thing that is in heaven above, or that is in
the earth beneath, or that is in the water under the earth. Thou
shalt not bow down thyself to them, nor serve them ... .

III. Thou shalt not take the name of the
Lord thy God in vain ... .

IV. Remember the sabbath day, to keep it holy.
Six days shalt thou labour, and do all thy work:
but the seventh day is the sabbath of the Lord thy God: in it
thou shalt not do any work... .

V. Honour thy father and thy mother: that thy days may be
long upon the land... .

VI. Thou shalt not kill.

VII. Thou shalt not commit adultery.

VIII. Thou shalt not steal.

IX. Thou shalt not bear false witness against thy neighbour.

X. Thou shalt not covet thy neighbour's house,
thou shalt not covet thy neighbour's wife, nor his manservant,
nor his maidservant, nor his ox, nor his ass, nor any thing
that is thy neighbour's [Exodus 20:2–17].

The Neo-Pagan Ten "Commandments"

1. Thou art God/dess.

2. As above, so below; as within so without.

3. Spirit abides in all things; words & names have power.

4. Maintain an attitude of gratitude (walk the talk).

5. Honor the ancestors, teachers, elders, and leaders.

6. All life is sacred.

7. All acts of love and pleasure are sacred.

8. Whatever you send out returns threefold.

9. Love is the law, love under will.

10. For the greatest good, an' it harm none.

Preface

Think Globally, Act Locally—Religious Ethics in Review

———————•◆◆◆•———————

*I came to the conclusion long ago . . . that all religions were true,
and also that all had some error in them—Mahatma Gandhi*

efore we start looking at a Witch's Ten Commandments
as compared to the Judeo-Christian Ten Commandments,
it would be helpful to review some of the world's major religions
and the basic ethical guidelines associated with them. Even vision-
based faiths do not exist in isolation. The way people of other faiths
live their ideals is part of what shapes what they believe and what
we believe about them. On some points we agree; on others we
disagree. However, during an era when Muslims do not recognize
Judaism as a religion, when Jews do not recognize Jesus as the Mes-
siah, when Protestants do not recognize the pope as the leader of
the Christian faith, and many Christian fundamentalists consider
Neo-Paganism as satanic, it seems pragmatic (if not urgently necessary) to ask, without judgment: *what makes us similar to each other,
rather than different?*

I think we will quickly discover there are underlying similarities—keys that unlock some of the answers to important

questions in the human condition. What is it, for example, that drives our need for faith? What rules of living do a majority of people hold dear? Do most people trust in an afterlife or a deity? How does this affect daily thoughts and actions?

Yes, this sounds a bit like trying to put "the meaning of life" in a nutshell. However, it's not quite as complex as that. As my husband often says, "The true meaning of life is that you're not dead yet, which also means we have yet more time to get this whole living thing right!" In this case, we're just looking at one area of life, our ethical foundations, not simply as a subculture, but as part of a greater whole.

Christianity

Since the title and structure for this book were based initially on Judeo-Christian concepts (the Ten Commandments), it seems appropriate to tackle the subject of Christianity first. Many Neo-Pagans started out with Judeo-Christian families and roots, either being brought up in a Christian home or having practiced as Christians for many years. This has created an inner struggle for some in our community in terms of handling the criticism of Neo-Paganism from some Christian factions, in terms of easing fears and concerns of family or friends, and in terms of coping with any residual negativity toward a religious system that simply left a person wanting (for whatever reason).

I am among those kept waiting, having grown up Lutheran and then finding my way to the Pentecostal Church during high school. For a while, the celebratory spirit of the latter seemed to fill a huge gap in my life. It gave me a place to be and belong. However, as I got older and began experiencing more of the world, I wanted to figure out personally what God had to say about God, not just what people had to say about this being. So I began to look inward, upward, and outward as well as studying many faiths. As you might imagine, this desire was met with criticism and on-going warnings of damnation.

It took time for me to forgive my critics, but then I realized that these people were only telling me what they truly believed. In fact, they were doing what their faith asked of them (i.e., "walking their talk").

When speaking of Christians the first set of guidelines most of us think about is the Ten Commandments that appear at the beginning of this book. Among these commandments are principles that tie into common global laws—like those regarding theft and murder. We also notice that some commandments (the tenth, for example) speak to the social mind of humankind in an effort to teach the best possible focus, in this case where to best direct one's attention (by showing that the proverbial grass isn't always greener on the other side).

The Ten Commandments are just the beginning of Christian guidelines and ethics. Rather, we must take a leap into the New Testament and review the teachings of Jesus. The message of Jesus was love—toward self, toward others, toward the earth, toward God. The New Testament also shows Jesus talking about:

Finding the kingdom of heaven in the now

The ability of faith to transform behavior from inside out

The importance of faith-based community (fellowship)

The blessings for those who make peace, show mercy, and remain faithful in the face of difficulties.

It's in these teachings that we see commonalities with a variety of faiths, including Neo-Pagan traditions. We would be hard pressed, for example, to find Neo-Pagan believers who say their faith does not change them, that they do not find fellowship helpful, and that peace and mercy are not admirable qualities that often manifest in wonderful ways.

Judaism

Because Judaism is the root religion of Christianity, it's not surprising to find some similarities in teachings. For example, both religions are officially monotheistic. The creator of the universe is God (YHWH), a being with whom one can develop a personal relationship. And while Neo-Pagans have many deities, many people would agree that a relationship with a deity is not only possible but also important to our faith and its practices.

The Jewish tradition is one that seeks to bring holiness into daily life, just as Neo-Pagans seek to bring spirituality into their daily life. A Jew is duty-bound to take care of himself or herself, both physical health and outward things like wearing the proper clothing. He or she is also instructed to act in good faith with neighbors, nurture friendships, strive for peace, and show benevolence and charity.

Jewish tradition is thus strongly based in a sense of community, not simply a person's local community but his spiritual community as well. As we read Jewish prayer books, we cannot help but notice the use of the terms "we" or "our" instead of "I" or "mine." This shows the importance of community. This is another point of commonality with those of us walking a Neo-Pagan path.

Jewish beliefs also show a strong family theme that revolves around the home and brings generations of family members together to celebrate common beliefs. In particular, monogamy and honoring one's parents are important. In times like ours when the strength of the family is often undermined, this is an important focus that supports both current and future generations, especially in terms of maintaining religious traditions.

Both within and outside the family, Jews regard personal integrity as a highly valued trait. Stealing, lying, taking advantage of innocence or ignorance, and oppression are forbidden. While this describes the way *people* should treat each other, it also extends to animals and to the earth. Gaia-ethically speaking, in this Neo-Paganism and Judaism seem to agree.

Taoism

When we move from Western to Eastern thinking, we notice a more philosophical approach to religion. Many of the concepts of Eastern religions can be applied outside their religious context. Sometimes people in the West find this confusing, but any time there's a divide in culture, it's not surprising to find a similar divide in religion and ethics.

Tao means simply "the way." This way is eternal. It cannot end because the human spirit (energy) cannot be destroyed. This way cannot be precisely defined because it's experiential. It is within and without all things. When we look at the world around us, however, it's obvious that things are way out of balance. So what's happened to the Tao?

Human actions, reactions, and inactions affect the overall balance of the world and of each individual in the world. The Tao gives us six keynotes based on that awareness of how our presence changes our world and the future with the goal being restoring and fulfilling our spirits. The first is *selflessness*. This doesn't mean destroying one's ego. Rather, it means being able to see yourself as part of a much greater whole, a whole that you're always affecting in some way. This is approximately what Neo-Pagans call being part of life's network in a responsible way.

The second keynote is *moderation*. If we look at the world honestly, limitations certainly exist. Real freedom, therefore, is discovering how far we can reach within the limitations presented. When we live in moderation, everything above and below that moderate point remains accessible to us. From the Neo-Pagan perspective, this translates into the idea of being true to self and setting reasonable goals in both mundane and spiritual matters. Serenity comes when we build foundations for those proverbial castles in the air.

The third keynote of Tao is *embracing the mystery*. This is where the Tao tackles our fears by saying there are some things we simply do not know and will likely never know. To be afraid accomplishes nothing. Taoists see this mystery as a kind of game that makes everything more fun (the ultimate "universal surprise," if you will). Overall the idea is to balance fear (which also can keep you from harming yourself) with healthy curiosity so that each individual continues to seek out his or her fullest potential. I would boil this down to what many Neo-Pagans profess: To Know, To Will, To Dare, To Be Silent.

The fourth Taoist keynote is *noncontrivance*. This is a little more difficult to explain. Tao sees that fixed plans and concepts do more harm than good. For example, if you have more weapons, you're actually less secure. If you have more money, you're likely to be less self-reliant. The more religious structure you bring to your life, the less spiritual and peaceful your life becomes. In short, we're instructed that we do not need to control the flow of Tao, even though we often think that living is all about trying to control everything.

The fifth keynote is *detachment*. Everyone is attached to something—some to action, some to apathy, some to anger, some to the pursuit of bliss, some to simple survival. Tao, however, says that life is a cycle and cannot simply be won or lost. This, of course, leads us to moderation. Anything that you attach yourself to in excess brings imbalance elsewhere. For example, the workaholic has forgotten how to play, but he may seek outrageous (even dangerous) forms of play to balance out that space in his life that's lacking. Basically, detachment says we should learn the difference between wants and needs, and then act fairly based on our understanding.

Last of all, we come to *humility*. This isn't quite what most Westerners think it is. Humility in this context is committing yourself to each moment equally, being content in yourself, and releasing the need for approval from others. Humility equates to self-acceptance, to being aware of purpose and place in all things. When we think about how big the universe is, it's easy to see how humility would arise in our thoughts.

Hinduism

Hindu ethics, as outlined by the sacred writings of the Vedas, begin at the hearth and home. This is something that Neo-Pagans can really relate to in that most of us consider our homes to be our temple. Each Hindu householder is encouraged to study the

Vedas, worship the gods, honor his ancestors, be kind to animals, and show hospitality. I think those guidelines are pretty sound for any spiritual being (with the minor adjustment of studying whatever sacred text you follow).

There are additional underlying considerations to Hindu ethics. First is *honesty*—speaking the truth. This truth is a tenuous thing, because while being truthful one must not betray a promise or confidence. This is a valuable goal, but one that's difficult to fulfill in a superficial society.

The second consideration in ethical Hinduism is *honoring life's journey in ritual*. From birth to death and other significant moments in between, Hindus see ritual as a kind of sacrament that sanctifies life's experiences. We see something similar in Neo-Paganism in rituals such as Wiccaning and rites of passage to adulthood, handfasting, and eldership (such as croning or saging).

Third comes a litany of "good" actions vs. "bad" actions that have some similarities to the Ten Commandments. Here we find advice like do not steal, covet, or lust; discipline your desires. We also find the encouragement to love others, to seek serenity, to remain steadfast during hardship, to cultivate devotion, and to act charitably without thought of reward.

Another part of the Hindu code of ethics manifests in vegetarianism. The general concept of nonviolence includes animals and fish because Hindus believe these creatures can be the host to a soul (as part of the cycle of reincarnation). This belief is coupled with sayings like, "When the diet is pure, the mind and heart are pure." Here, we see abstinence as something thought to have healthful benefits, even as the Jewish kosher codes were designed around a combination of religion and medicine.

Buddhism

Buddhism offers the Eightfold Path as a framework for effective spiritual (or philosophical) living. This path is divided into three parts. The first part inspires wisdom (right view and right intention). The second part represents core ethics (right speech, right action, right livelihood), and the third part focuses on mental development (right effort, right mindfulness, right concentration).

The greatest emphasis in Buddhism seems to be on practical living. For example, it's not thought that one can simply walk the Eightfold Path one step at a time and come to enlightenment. Rather, the principles of the path are interdependent principles that relate to and affect each other.

Beginning with the road to wisdom, we'll consider right view and right intention. Right view means the ability to see things in a different way. Instead of things being separate and independent, right view uses all the capacities of the human mind and insight to begin grasping the "bigger picture" (the macrocosm and microcosm, the as above, so below). Once that worldview forms, it will inevitably affect personal actions and thoughts.

Right intention is the energy behind action. Right intention commits itself to ethical self-improvement. Within this part of the path, there are three underlying distinguishers: resisting desire, resisting anger or aversion, and resisting violence and cruelty. Thus, right intention results in goodwill, peace, compassion, and selflessness. This ties into the idea of "the good of all" about which Neo-Pagans speak.

The core ethics of right speech, right action, and right livelihood tie into the first two. Right speech can make or break a life. Lies, slander, harshness, and idle chatter are considered unproductive and potentially harmful. One's words should be based in right view and right intention so the resulting speech is friendly, warm, and gentle.

Right action is physical. It's knowing when to act and when to be still. It's also a personal promise to abstain from harming others (specifically taking life, i.e., thou shall not kill), abstain from robbery or fraud (thou shall not steal or bear false witness), and abstain from sexual misconduct. In short, right action is about treating others with kindness, honesty, and compassion. It means respecting their personal property, and doing "no harm" in consensual relationships with others.

Right livelihood speaks to the way we earn our living. Money should be gained through legal, peaceful means, and any occupation that would cause a person to break with the rest of the Eightfold Path should be avoided. This part of the path can be quite difficult in a society where sometimes you have to "take what you can get" in terms of work. However, I think it behooves us to consider how we're spending our professional time, and how our jobs affect us spiritually.

Finally, we come to the mental development guidelines of right effort, right mindfulness, and right concentration. Effort is based in will, Neo-Pagans can consider the words, "love is the law, love under will," as we ponder this lesson. Misguided effort causes confusion, distraction, and can lead to unwholesome states like aggression and envy. Right effort tells us to be self-disciplined, honest, and kind.

Right mindfulness allows us to see things clearly and as they truly are (without rose-colored glasses). It strives to penetrate interpretive schemes and impressions without going astray. The goal of right mindfulness is helped greatly by meditation, being mindful of body, feelings, state of mind, and being able to contemplate things in a balanced manner.

Last is right concentration, which is also vastly aided by meditation. This is something many people have problems with because it's reeducating your mind to look at one point, one issue, one person, one concept at a time instead of hundreds (in other words, FOCUS). Right concentration asks us, to what do you give your attention and why? For any spiritual seeker, this is a good question that's well worth regular thought.

Islam

Sunni (but not Shia) Islam offers the Five Pillars as a means to put faith in action (walking the talk). The Five Pillars are (1) the profession of faith in Allah (God), (2) prayer, (3) the paying of alms, (4) fasting, and (5) the pilgrimage (Hajj) to Mecca.

The first Pillar is the *declaration of faith*. Specifically, "There is none worthy of worship except God and Muhammad is the messenger of God." This is comparable to the First Commandment.

The second pillar is *prayer*. There are five prescribed prayers that contain verses from the Qur'an and they can be offered at any time, though most Muslims typically pray at dawn, midday, late-afternoon, right after sunset, and one hour after sunset. In this regular rhythm, we see an effort to keep spirituality as a part of daily life (like many other faiths discussed in this chapter), and remain in constant connection with deity.

Before beginning to pray, Muslims ceremonially clean themselves. This is done so that they are physically free of "dirt"; many Neo-Pagans similarly take ritual baths to purify the aura and spirit as well as body. We see cleansing in other faiths, too, as most people believe that it's only proper to be clean before going before sacred powers. Hand in hand with cleansing comes the Fourth Pillar, *fasting*, which of course is also a purifier. By avoiding one earthy comfort, even for a short time, a person can focus more clearly on God.

The Third Pillar is *charity*. Muslims believe that wealth is given to people in trust. (As it is written in the New Testament, "for unto whomsoever much is given, of him shall be much required," Luke 12:48). When we give a portion to the needy and to society, our possessions are purified and, indeed, it encourages a new financial flow that is similar to karmic balance and the concept of giving to receive. It should be noted, however, that in Islam charity is not limited to funds. Kindness, a smile, physical assistance, etc., are all considered charitable.

Finally, all Muslims are encouraged to make at least one *pilgrimage* to Mecca if they are able, physically and financially. Pilgrims wear special clothes that eliminate distinctions of class and culture, making all pilgrims equal before God. Once there, the pilgrims join in prayer for forgiveness, then join in celebration to mark the occasion. The Baha'i and the Sikhs have similar customs, and people of all faiths have felt compelled to go on pilgrimage to sacred sites to feel more connected with their gods.

Baha'i

Baha'i teaches that each person has an immortal soul and that there is an underlying unity to the great religions of the world. While the religions do not hold exactly the same doctrines, their ethical values are often similar, and Baha'i sees them as having arisen from the same spiritual source. They also believe that throughout time this source sends teachers, from Krishna, Moses, and Jesus to guide humankind's path.

The core practices of the Baha'i are clear: to *pray* daily (this strengthens one's relationship with deity), *observe holy days*, *fast* regularly, *work* toward abolishing prejudice, see work as a form of worship (or, as I say, work is good magick), make at least one *pilgrimage* to the Shrine of the Bab if possible, and to not consume alcohol. This last prohibition reflects the Baha'i's early ties to Shiite Islam.

Confucianism

Confucianism is akin to Buddhism in that it's more a philosophical way of life than a religion, per se. This system has six central ideals to which followers strive to keep, and while the six can be taken separately as good advice for nearly anyone of any spiritual persuasion, they're intended to work cooperatively (which is similar to the Eightfold Path).

The first ideal is called Li. This includes things like the *necessity of propriety, etiquette, and the rituals of daily life*. Intertwined with Li we find Hsiao, the *love one should have toward their parents, and parents toward their children*. Both of these have been reflected repeatedly in the other beliefs we've examined thus far.

The third ideal is *righteousness*, followed by *honesty* and *trustworthiness*. This order makes complete sense. If one is "right" in spirit, the other two follow naturally.

The fifth ideal is the highest virtue in Confucian philosophy, that of Jen. Jen is *benevolence and humane treatment toward others*. In part it's "doing unto others," but more importantly "doing" because it's the right thing, not necessarily for some type of reward.

Last of all, Confucian ideals embrace a sense of *loyalty* to the state; many other faiths talk about praying for our leaders. (When I first read the sixth ideal I had to smile. No matter how enlightened we seem to be, politics infiltrates everything!)

Jainism

Jainism sees the universe as a series of layers that include heavens and hells. In the heavens, we find celestial beings and liberated souls. In the hells, we find places of punishment. Where one ends up depends on karma (the accumulated good or evil done in life). Complete liberation only comes from asceticism and seeking after enlightenment. After having raised their families and provided social services, many Jains become monks so they can focus wholly on enlightenment.

The five basic principles in Jainism begin in *nonviolence*, whether against a human, animal, or even a vegetable. Violence creates negative karma and adversely affects the quest for enlightenment. Building on that foundation, the second ideal is *honesty* and the idea that falsehoods should be avoided.

The third principle sets a *taboo against theft*, fourth is *monogamy*, and fifth is *detachment*. By detachment, Jainism teaches that excessive material possessions weigh down the soul; so does overindulgence. Combined with the idea of nonviolence, this is why most Jains are fruitarian (those who eat only those things that do not kill the plant or animal from which it comes, like nuts).

Shinto

There are four basic teachings in Shinto. The first is a focus on tradition and family. As in Judaism, it is believed that one's family is the mechanism through which tradition and history are preserved, specifically through rituals. Rituals to recognize birth and marriage are key. The second teaching is one that has strong Neo-Pagan overtones: the love of nature. The earth is a sacred thing, and the closer one comes to nature, the closer he or she comes to deity.

Shinto says that many elements of nature house spirits, called *kami*, and some are *kami* worshipped. The third teaching is *Matsuri*, the worship of *kami* and ancestral spirits. One determining factor in what may house a spirit seems to be its overall beauty, structure, and strength. For example, if a large rock has a vein of quartz running through it that looks like a trickle of water, that rock might be said to have a spirit. Likewise, a tree that stands firm after a terrible storm when others have fallen would likely be regarded as having a strong spirit. When a tree is cut down, its spirit must be appeased or honored.

Living in harmony with spirits is very important—not just the spirits that are important to a place or thing, but also those of other faiths. This harmony is so important that the Shinto religion is regarded as a very private affair, between you and the spirits. To ask anyone about matters of faith, or discuss it without express permission, is considered very rude.

The fourth teaching of Shinto is *cleanliness*. The washing of hands and rinsing of one's mouth are two habits adopted by Shinto practitioners.

Summary

We can see that people who have chosen the major spiritual, religious and philosophical paths seem to have some common ground. The elements that create that common ground include:

Contemplating the eternal nature of the soul (but not necessarily what happens to the soul after death)

Performing our proper duties toward God and your religion (though what constitutes god, or deity, may vary)

Acknowledging family and community responsibilities and values (fairly universal)

Accepting social and personal culpability (fairly universal, but for the forgiveness clause, which seems to be an "easy out" for bad behavior when misused)

Manifesting our faith or philosophy in our life. It should change us, or why bother? This is walking our talk in such a way as everyone, including us, can tell something is different.

Developing kindness, compassion, consideration, respect, honor, and gratitude (fairly universal)

Celebrating the journey of life in ritual (the rituals in religions all have moments that commemorate all that it is to be human)

It seems that no matter what country or era, human beings pretty much want the same things. We also seem to want good things that can make the world a better place. Once we can come together and focus on those things and begin to work for them collectively, it will be, as a Native American author wrote; "We will call the Earth by one name—Home." Let it be said . . . let it ring through human awareness . . . let it be done!

Introduction

Our scientific power has outrun our spiritual power.
We have guided missiles and misguided men.
—Martin Luther King Jr.

The Neo-Pagan movement is arguably the most diversified and vision-driven faith in all of history. Soul searching, frustrated with carved-in-stone ideals, and expressing a need for personal expression, Neo-Pagans are typically liberal-minded folk who embrace diversity and openness with ardent passion. As some have said, we are people of heart, not of a book.

Yet, the growing number of people involved with New Age schools and churches, the way the study of New Age blends ancient and modern beliefs, and the fact that Wicca became more publicly recognized over sixty years ago presents an interesting challenge for many people, myself included. For those of us who desire something that will withstand the test of time, how do we establish a book, a framework, that provides those within and without the Craft with a sense of who we are at heart? This is no small task.

If we want Neo-Paganism to continue thriving, we must begin creating basic constructs somewhere. Our society is one that demands some sense of structure; black and white outlines, if you will (even if we end up coloring outside those lines). Without a semblance of structure, the public will continue to regard many New Age belief systems (into which Neo-Paganism is typically lumped) nothing more than fads, which (in turn) severely hampers our capacity to have a respected voice among world religions.

As an additional challenge to that structure, we must understand that the popular and mainstream religions won't just suddenly transform to become whatever people wish them to be (through revisionist history or whatever). Individuals who have a long-held tradition tend to treasure it, and with good reason. The collective culture of each faith, how it was practiced, and how the gods were worshipped are essential elements that need to be pondered no matter how we've adapted that path to our reality and modern world. How do we bridge the gap between tradition, culture, and history and what is truly practicable today?

While it's impossible to discuss all the variables in one book, the goal of *A Witch's 10 Commandments* is to open up our broomclosets to serious ethical and moral scrutiny. In the pages of this book, we'll consider some of the issues that lie heavily on the minds of people in our community—questions such as, can we bring our children up in a magickal tradition without overriding free will? To what type of accountability can we hold our priests, priestesses, and other leaders? Should we consider having paid clergy like other faiths?

A Witch's 10 Commandments also considers the questions and issues that affect our community from the political, social, and familial sectors. Politically speaking, how do we protect our freedom of religion in the face of church-state lines being crossed? Socially, how do we support alternative lifestyles that the public hasn't fully embraced? And for our families, just explaining that we're a pagan, Wiccan, Druid, or shaman or whatever can prove to be an emotional and difficult undertaking that often leaves feelings of guilt or creates distance between us and our loved ones. These issues, and many others, affect us dramatically every day. It's time we stopped dancing around them with flowery language (or worse, avoiding them altogether) and started getting down to brass tacks.

What are the basics? The answers are who we are individually and collectively, what types of ideology the broad-based Neo-Pagan movement encompasses. Believe it or not, there are some similarities to be found here. For example, you'll be hard pressed to find a Neo-Pagan who doesn't have a strong respect for the earth. In fact, most are very ecologically oriented. This kind of underlying commonality is part of what this book examines.

Going one step further, *A Witch's 10 Commandments* ponders our diversity and its effects on individuals joining our communities or those being raised among them. To help with this process, I have interviewed several Neo-Pagan leaders around the United States and asked for their assistance in lending wisdom and insight to these pages. For this book to begin to speak to the heart of the all, it must have more than one voice. I am very grateful for the voices that have tried to guide me in this undertaking.

Now before all this sounds too lofty, please know that unlike tablets from Zion, this book is not engraved in stone. It has often been said that trying to get Neo-Pagans to wholly agree on anything is akin to herding cats. That is the nature of an individually-centered visionary faith. However, I don't think it's unreasonable to believe there is something that brings us together in fellowship . . . to believe there are some things we're willing to fight for . . .

to believe we can, indeed, build on some type of common ground so that our future will be more secure.

That belief also means that I may unwittingly step on some toes in the pages ahead. If the resulting antagonism, disagreement, shock, or other conflicting emotions cause us to pause and really think, really consider our ethics and our foundations, and more importantly do something productive about them, then there's no need for apology. There's no expectation here of becoming a guru or trying to set up an absolute authority. The only expectation is that of an honest exploration––personally and communally––of those very things that are the heart and soul of any religion. If we achieve that, it will be a huge step forward.

The real focus of *A Witch's 10 Commandments* boils down to what will inspire us to be the best human beings possible–at home, at work, on the road, in circle, in our tribes/communities, and as citizens of the world. Truly, that is the whole reason to examine ethics and morals anyway: to learn from our past, both the darkness and the light, so we can build toward a better future. This book is only one step in that process, and it ultimately begins in your own spirit when you say, "Yes, I am ready."

If you are nodding right now, then come and join me in the pages of this book. We'll explore Wicca, Paganism, and associated beliefs together and possibly find completely different answers to our questions, but at least we will *find* them.

Commandment 1

The Judeo-Christian First Commandment says, I am the Lord thy God, which have brought thee out of the land of Egypt, out of the house of bondage. Thou shalt have no other gods before me.

Neo-Paganism teaches, Thou art God/dess.

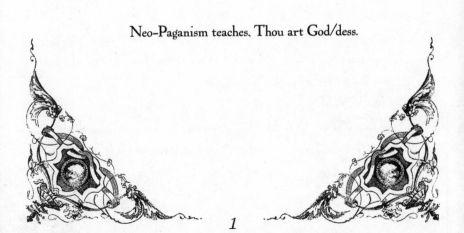

n the beginning, silence was deafening. Darkness twisted and turned relentlessly in an empty, turbulent sea, anticipating the time when it would no longer be alone. No matter Darkness's wishes, change remained slow and methodical in its movements, seeming to take an eternity. So the darkness waited patiently in solitude.

Finally, after eons, from the depths of the indigo silence, came a whisper. All but imperceptible at first, it grew outward on a wave that transformed the night into an ocean of promise. In the center of the swell, a small spark appeared from which stars, planets, and galaxies poured forth endlessly, gloriously, joyfully filled with potentials beyond compare. Darkness would never be alone again.

Thousands of years later (but a second in infinity), the winds of change blew across a blue planet, and the Wheel of Life began to spin. Molecule to molecule, link to link, web to web, it reached outward. Following its motion, the earliest creatures crawled from their homes in the deep. This had been their safe womb, but another voice above the waves beckoned, the voice of the soil.

On and on, the great Wheel turned. With it, these beings grew and changed, shaped by the hand of time. As their minds expanded, they began to think about the "spirits" in nature; the call of the wind, the strength of the sun, the fury of storms. How could humankind touch such awesome powers? This macrocosm, this superconscious, was vast. Would the cries for insight be heard above the swell?

The Wheel kept inching forward, bringing constant transformation. As philosophers in every culture began walking sand strewn paths, they provided many outlooks to consider. Ardent seekers everywhere listened

intently, hoping to find universal truths within the words. Yet, the words were somehow wanting. External truth, it seemed, was illusive and prone to opinion, prone to politics and era, prone to personal consciousness. Nonetheless, undaunted, the Wheel spun onward and another cycle began.

Later still, idealists, dreamers, and visionaries looked within. There they found the same spirits, the same spark that existed without. Symbols were sought to express this knowledge; the cup or grail, the sword, the staff or rod, the coin or pentacle, each provided one part of a greater picture. Yet, again, this picture was incomplete. The tools were lifeless, and unlike the Earth they lay sleeping at the Seeker's fingers waiting for expression.

When the Wheel moves again, the voices gain volume; the voices from nature that have always been here. It has been millions of years now; years of being deaf to this ageless canticle, blind to the power of the Earth, and unable to express the message in the waves. Yet the symphony sings on, knowing that there will be a few special people in each generation who hear and heed the call. It is time to answer.

Finally, the Fool turns to the world, turns to the time-not-time, lying aside outmoded notions, and ready to make the leap of faith. There, stretched expectantly before the Seeker, are all the secrets, all the power of creation, all the tools ever needed by humankind. In the song of a bird, the murmurs of a volcano, the groan of a sprouting seedling, and yes, the music of the ocean . . . our ancient home.

Today, the Seeker returns to the Monad and to the Sacred Self, listening intently to the voice of eternity. Here to attain vision; here to retrieve truth.

Thou Art God/dess

Wᵍhile you might not feel much like one first thing in the morning before your shower and a coffee, thou art God/dess. This powerful aspect of spirit resides within each person. Wondering why you've never heard that before? It's a realization to which we are only now reawakening. Throughout human history we have often lost sight of the divine. Various things caused our temporary blindness, from technological advances to human ego or apathy. Nonetheless, no matter how far we tried to shove the God/dess into a societal, mental, or spiritual abyss, this potent force never left our side or our awareness. Just look at the continued reverence toward the Mother Mary and emerging Goddess art to verify this truth. Despite changing times and shifting cultural approval, the Goddess found a way to remain a part of human awareness.

Ah, but let's back up for a moment. Why this particular spelling—*god/dess*? Because many Witches and Neo-Pagans see spirit as having both masculine and feminine energies (being both and neither). Additionally, deity is not something that just sits off in the astral realm making bets on what humankind will do next. In effect, deity is part of all things, just as a parent's DNA evidences itself in a child. That doesn't mean the sacred parent (or parents, depending on your perspective) has no personality, but rather it must embrace all facets of human diversity in itself as the root of all our characteristics and uniqueness.

So what exactly does this mean ethically to Wiccans? I believe we have to look at this question from two perspectives. The first is the divine outside of the self, and the second is the divine as part of self and all creation.

Relationship with the Monad or Deity/Deities

In talking to both monotheistic and polytheistic Neo-Pagans one thing becomes very clear. They typically strive to develop a viable relationship with whatever gods and goddesses they've chosen, and also strive to keep the lines of communication open in that relationship. The methods for that communication include prayer, ritual, and meditation, each of which we'll talk about briefly later.

The question becomes why? If "thou art God/dess," why cultivate an external relationship? Esoteric philosophy gives us hints to the answer for this question by telling us that each person's soul is an expression of divine thought and actually a small spark of the eternal fire (the Monad). That spark gives us the capacity (and the desire) to seek out the greater fire, and to know it intimately, albeit on a smaller scale that our minds can handle. And, as we interact with that fire, the hope would be that our own godspark grows to the point of enlightenment, where we can rejoin our spirit with the One.

Now, before you feel like you're back in philosophy class, let's put this in simpler terms; returning to the more familiar terms of a parent-child relationship. Children are part of the family (a Monad unit), but they are also unique individuals. Children will seek out the Monad, especially the key figures in it, naturally, and they'll also often rebel against those figures (as part of the learning process). It's really no different for Neo-Pagans in their interaction with gods or goddesses.

The polytheistic Neo-Pagan develops relationships with various beings (personalities), each of which represents something that draws the believer's heart and spirit into communion. Perhaps it's a cultural connection, perhaps it's situational, perhaps the being came to that person in a dream, or they had an intense ritual experience involving that personality. Whatever the reason, the way we "see" each god or goddess is still only a small fragment simply because we are mortal and are looking at the universe from a limited perspective.

The monotheistic Neo-Pagan sees all the names and faces of deity as part of a greater whole (akin to facets of a crystal). You can direct your attention to any single part of that crystal (Isis, Zeus, Ishtar, Ra, etc.), focusing on that part's attributes and abilities, but you are always mindful that you're dealing with one tiny segment of something much bigger. Neither of these ways of seeing the divine is "right" or "wrong," It is simply the way in which humans have re-created god in our image, and in a way that seems to make sense in our reality.

Having said that, ethically speaking, the reason why one would conscientiously work on developing an external relationship with deity is:

✝ To begin internalizing the positive attributes of that deity in the hopes of working toward spiritual fulfillment,

✝ To improve self-awareness and self-actualization (i.e., by coming to know the divine without, you can recognize and activate it within), and

✝ So as to not be asking for assistance from a deity who is, essentially, a stranger.

All these reasons are very important.

As spiritual beings, we have a responsibility to ourselves, to others, and to the fabric of all things to diligently work on self-improvement. When you see life as a network, one person in that tapestry does, indeed, make a difference to the whole picture. The best way to remain culpable and involved in that tapestry is to look to the ultimate in development (to deity) and do our best to epitomize that being. It stands to reason that such exemplification cannot happen if you don't *know* him or her.

In terms of asking for help, that's an age-old tradition that's perfectly normal between parents and children (as well as between lower self and higher self). When you're in trouble, confused, or uncertain of the way, you go to an authority figure for help. In this case, the authority is the divine. However, it's rather unseemly to just show up on God's proverbial doorstep looking for a handout when you've never even introduced yourself.

As in any relationship, you have to put some effort forward to see any "rewards" from the interaction. If you treat your gods with love, devotion, and respect, that is what you will receive in return, just like with a spouse. If you treat your gods as a convenient combination of Santa Claus and something to do while you're bored, that's how they'll treat you in return—along with some malice for making them feel like the butt of a joke (again, just like a spouse). Thankfully, from what I've experienced, the divine does indeed meet us halfway, and the internal divine provides a compass to guide us to that mark.

Getting to Know God/dess: Connecting with (and Staying Connected with) Deity

If we're going to begin fostering your relationship with deity, the next step is pondering the means by which to accomplish that goal. The three most common methods for bridging the gap between a person and God are meditation, ritual, and prayer. These can be used together or separately, but we'll look at them individually so you can determine which approach will work best for your path and vision.

Meditation

What do you think when you hear the word "meditate"? Sitting with your legs tied up like a pretzel? If so, fear not. Meditation is more a state of mind than body, and in fact, mind-over-matter is only part of the goal. However, it should be noted that the desired effect of meditation depends much on with what foundational system you begin. For example, the monk from the Far East might meditate to free himself from all thoughts by walking or other forms of exercise. In that part of the world, meditation isn't always sedentary.

Eye of the Beholder— Visions of Deity

If you do not have a clear vision of the divine, now is an excellent time to start thinking about that being and what he/she/it will mean in your spiritual journey. Journaling is a great way to sort out your thoughts about God/dess and to also begin organizing your feelings about the godself within.

In the West, a physician might recommend meditation to a patient to alleviate stress and help regulate blood pressure. A Sufi dancer spins in a circle as a way of focusing inward and upward and becoming one with deity. Neo-Pagans might use a quiet meditation (together or alone) to integrate lessons and ideas so they can manifest outwardly in viable and comprehensible ways.

All those potential motivations aside, we want to concentrate on meditation as a tool to reconnect with, and stay connected to, deity (both within and without). For those who get frustrated when they try to meditate, try thinking about it differently. Instead of seeing it as a chore, think about it like you do those times when you lose yourself to a book or an activity you love. When indulging yourself in these relaxing hobbies, time seems to go by unnoticed. Sometimes you don't recognize people around you coming and going, and if someone asks you a question, it's likely to go unanswered or get a simple, "uh huh." That type of focus is meditation. You really can do this.

How can you use this focus to connect with deity? Well, if you're a very physical person, take a brisk walk or dance to calm your mind and hone in on deity. If you're a tactile person, wear something comfortable when you meditate. If you're visual, get a picture or statue of the sacred parent that sends your spirit soaring every time you see it. If you love sound, play music that somehow resonates with the vision of deity you hold in your heart. The human spirit has great potential, but our mind is the part of our being that must take what seems "so big" and interpret it in ways we can grasp. Therefore working with sensual cues becomes a bridging mechanism. It breaches the gap between mundane and magickal, temporal and eternal.

Symbolically speaking, that's also the way in which deity will communicate—through icons you can understand. It's interesting to note that the most common time during which people receive some form of communication from deity is when they're asleep. Why? Because when we're awake we're so busy and our world is so filled with noise, it's about the only time the sacred parent can get a word in edgewise. Meditation provides another opportunity for stillness so that you can hear that still small voice within and without.

If meditation has proven difficult for you, don't feel alone. It's very common to be frustrated at first. You are retraining your mind to quiet all the things that normally float around in that proverbial holding bin, and turn its attention toward one thing, God/dess. So you're likely to find that one itch you cannot scratch, one muscle will cramp up, you'll think of all the stuff you should have done (and forgot until now), etc. That's why meditation is considered a practice. It takes time to get it right.

Some simple things have proven helpful to many people of numerous spiritual varieties. These include:

✝ **Steady, paced breathing.** Throughout time, breath has been likened to the wind of God, and now you can take that concept one step further by recognizing deity with every breath you take. Slow and evenly, breathe in and out so that the end of one breath becomes the beginning of the next.

✝ **Listening to your heartbeat.** The heart has often been considered the seat of the soul metaphorically. Thus, your heartbeat is the pulse of God and the universe. The rhythm, when blended with breath, makes a symphony that's unique to you, yet connected to all things.

✝ **Posture and privacy.** On a more mundane level, make sure you're comfortable and assure yourself of some privacy. Start out slowly at first, just five minutes. As you find your body and mind resisting less and less, increase the amount of time that you meditate.

Within a month or two, most people find that they can meditate for about fifteen minutes a day without too much difficulty. Think of it like taking a spiritual vitamin. It's not only good for your soul, it's good for the body, too.

Honoring Your Journey

Find meaningful ways to regularly honor your journey in a way that feeds your soul, both where you've come from and where you hope to go. Remember to pat yourself on the back for accomplishments and continue to focus on those things you're trying to change. In particular, consider using special days (your birthday is ideal) as a time to bring these things back to your thoughts and meditations. However, I personally believe that once a year is not enough to internalize and recognize all of our ongoing changes. I recommend at least once every quarter, perhaps at the changing of the seasons.

Ritual

Next, let's consider ritual as a helpmate. To many Neo-Pagans, ritual isn't simply about illustrating a particular season, idea, or goal. Instead, it's about completion, fulfillment, and manifestation. Through ritual (as through prayer and meditation), we consummate our relationship with the spiritual world. It's interesting to note that linguistically the root word for "ritual" means "fit together." In this case, we are learning to fit together our human nature with that of the divine.

Now, before you start envisioning pews and rote invocations, ritual is a vital, living thing. It can be playful or serious, but it is not stagnant nor is it something with which you're unfamiliar. Human life is full of ritual, but a great deal of that is centered on everyday life. For example, many people follow a morning ritual (a repeated pattern of actions), and when they cannot do this, the whole day seems off somehow. In a spiritual construct we use a specific pattern of words and actions to create an atmosphere of sacredness, one more conducive to reminding us of our inner divinity, one that supports our relationship with the divine.

Since one of the goals of Wicca is to be the magickal, life itself can become a sacred ritual. It's just a matter of attitude and awareness. Yes, it takes time to manifest that kind of ongoing connection, and there will be those "off" days when deity seems very far away indeed. There will also be times when you want to create or use a special ritual for more specific purposes. However, if you strive to pattern your life as an act of worship, you can't go too far astray.

For those times in which you do want a more formal ritual, the key elements to success include:

‡ A specific opening that helps the participants adjust from mundane thinking to spiritual be-ing

‡ Having a setting and props that sensually support the working's (the magickal ritual or method) goals (such as images of deity if you're working on energy for communion such as drawing down the moon)

‡ Activities that likewise support the goal (prayer, meditation, spells, chants, etc.)

‡ Allowing for intuitive changes and spirit's input

‡ A recognizable closing and time to ground

‡ Opportunity to integrate the experience through journaling, talking, etc.

‡ Making note of what worked best, and using those things again. (The more you use a successful approach, the more ritualized it becomes and the more positive energy it creates so long as it remains truly meaningful.)

This last point cannot be stressed enough. If we allow our faith to become nothing more than rote movement and words, the magick will die. There must be a spirit-mind-heart connection in ritual, and indeed in all of life, if we want our faith to grow in viable ways. That also means ongoing effort must replace complacency in how we talk about, teach about, and deal with religious issues in our community, not the least of which is our freedom to worship in ritual. Later in the book, we will be talking about ethics and social action, but it's good to start thinking about it now (specifically, how it may affect the long-term stability of our community).

Prayer

Prayer is not simply an action. To me it is also an attitude (of prayerfulness). From this perspective, prayerfulness (like ritual) is a means to draw sacred energies into daily life. Prayerfulness means living reverently and respectfully. And where meditation tends to be an inner conversation, prayer reaches outward.

Prayer can be expression of desire and perceived need that gives us the opportunity to remember that we are not alone in, or in creating, the universe. As part of something larger than ourselves, we have greater resources than we have as individuals. Coming to this understanding helps us realize and have faith that there is undoubtedly more than one way to meet our needs and satisfy our wants, express thanks, and invoke spirit into our daily reality.

In any case, because Neo-Pagans liken prayer to a spell, ethically, it becomes a bit of a sticky wicket. Spellcraft stresses the importance of avoiding manipulation, yet most people don't stop to think about the implications of the things for which they're asking through prayer. Prayer is a form of communication, and the energies created by it have to balance divine will, personal will, and universal law into a functional pattern, which is why we don't always get the response we want. To help understand this predicament a bit better, let's look at a specific situation. Say someone's having financial trouble.

Step One: Before praying for money, the first ethical question is whether he or she has made viable efforts on the mundane level to rectify that situation. If not, the results from prayer are likely to be wanting. As our own priest and priestess, we must stop and invoke the divine within and be ready to *do* something so that the universe has more opportunities to create the transformation for which we hope. Action opens doors and engenders energy.

Step Two: Using this same scenario, consider what that individual is willing to offer or sacrifice to help the situation. Praying for the "gimme" without being willing to release or do anything isn't the answer here. There are very real sacrifices to be made to ensure that the balance of energies is maintained. Don't expect the universe to do all the work. Hard work is good magick, and it's also a mechanism through which we learn and grow.

Step Three: Consider needs versus wants. We can certainly ask for things we want in prayer, but things that we truly *need* are ultimately a priority. For example, you may want medical insurance to feel more secure, but it won't just get handed to you. What you *need* is a job to pay for that medical insurance. An awareness of wants versus needs (and defining them in specific terms) can help sort out the form of prayer. Your offering then becomes one of giving up personal time—working to meet that need.

Step Four: Welcome and allow help from deity. Deity won't just stomp all over your reality. Sometimes, when we have prayed for something, we expect a direct and explicit response to our request. For example, if a woman prays for the love of her life to stay with her forever, she may be surprised and disappointed when her significant other ends their relationship a week later. However, further down the road, she may discover that her prayers were answered when she meets a new man who proves to be the love of her life, although not the one she had in mind when praying for her life partner. Was it the answer she was expecting? Not really, but it was the answer she was given (and likely an answer with much more longevity). It's very rude to throw away gifts from the universe, especially blessings for which one asks. What we think is best for us often isn't, and our blessings therefore sometimes arrive in odd wrappings. It may take a while to understand divine logic, but over time the whole reason for your personal circumstances will become evident. Allow it to happen!

With this example in mind, it's good to pray and meditate often to keep the lines of communication open. *Only ask for help*, however, when you come to the end of yourself and your viable options or to support those "hands on" actions by way of guidance. This is each person's responsibility as a cocreator in reality.

How about a different ethical example that's not so personal, like praying for someone else's health? Overall, it's never really wrong to want good things for others, including healing, or to try to restrain someone from self-harm. The difficulty here is that we live in an imperfect world and have imperfect or incomplete knowledge. Our limited vision often cannot perceive the potential harm or good from any such healing prayers. However, if we constantly allow that limitation to hinder action, nothing will ever get done. If you do nothing when you *feel* you should do something, ethically, that memory will be answerable to your inner god-self. Guilt is not productive or helpful. The person in need of healing is you. Similarly, acting when you feel you *should not act* creates inner turmoil. The best answer here is to trust your instincts: trust that small voice within, and if you choose to act, then do so with wisdom as a guide.

In this illustration, Neo-Pagan ethics demand some type of clause that puts our humanness and its potential errors into the hands of the universe. Even if "thou art God/dess," that's a part of ourselves we're only really starting to rediscover and know. So, when you release the energy of a prayer, word it in such a way that a person can accept or reject that energy, and include some expression to guide the energy in the best possible manner. For many of us, the words *"let this work for the greatest good and harm none"* (or some derivative) handles that part of the equation we cannot see or know. It is a sound, principled approach to all prayers

Relationship Building

If you have already chosen a personal god or goddess (or several), put aside a specific amount of time in your regular schedule (daily, weekly, or monthly) to study him, her, or them. Find out about special holidays that center around those beings, also about the things they hold sacred. This is part of the relationship building process.

Relationship with the God-self

Someone once joked with me, saying that since "thou art God/dess," praying is like talking to yourself. (I, of course, answered, "That way I only hear what I really like!") Seriously, however, in our relationship building process with deity, we cannot overlook the fact that part of this life adventure's goal is to "know thyself" and become self-responsible. If a spark of deity resides within, self-awareness will, in turn, naturally help external efforts to remain connected with the divine fires. Yes, it sounds like circular reasoning, but it is the rule of *as within, so without* on a very intimate level.

The first step in this process, in my opinion, is accepting two things: your role as a cocreator in your destiny, and your role as a priest or priestess in your spiritual life. There is a tendency in immature souls to make excuses for bad behavior or blame other people or situations for problems—anything to avoid actual responsibility. This is normal, and certainly easier, but does nothing for us in terms of our quest for enlightenment, let alone empowering ourselves to live ethically.

What (if anything) should we do about wavering, floundering souls, especially if we're among them? First of all, I favor the idea of cleaning up our own act before we go around telling anyone else how to live (personally, communally, and globally). To do anything less causes us to stumble into that nasty disorder called hypocrisy, which could easily lead to a fall into the guru trap, which we'll discuss shortly. It is all well and good to be able to recognize positives and negatives. It's another thing altogether to go around destructively critiquing other peoples' flaws, especially when you have similar ones.

Step One, then, is some honest personal appraisal. One activity that may help you with this is writing up two lists. On one list, write all the things in your life that you feel the need to improve on. For example, perhaps you have a harsh temper or tend to procrastinate. Those negative traits go on page one. Be brutally honest with yourself! On the other list, write down those things that you're good at with similar nonreservation. To prioritize, you may want to put an asterisk next to the ones that really strike you as being harmonious with your inner God-self. This isn't the time to be humble or overly sensitive: *know thyself.*

Next, prioritize that list. Which of the negatives do you feel are most important to change initially? Be reasonable in your expectations regarding those things you feel you can improve. For example, it's reasonable to want to improve your employability, but it may require going back to school or taking some other training. Can you find a way to fit that into your current schedule? If so, then it's reasonable to put it toward the top of your "work-in-progress" list. Next, prioritize the positives. Be happy regarding those things about which you are the most proud. Afterward, start working on item one on the "bad" list conscientiously and diligently. Ideally, you could take proactive strides toward improvement every day. At the same time, start sharing or using item one on the "good" list. This creates a potent symmetry. The "good" gift that you're applying provides positive energy that can be applied toward self-empowerment to change those things you're not happy with. Once you start this process, you'll find it comes more naturally.

Mind you, there will be "off" days. Be as patient with yourself as you'd be with others, if not more. Rome wasn't built in a day, and no soul was ever born getting it all right all the time, from their birth onward. Step by step, transformation by transformation, use this cooperative balance to make your way through the wilderness. In time, you'll find that you're able to help provide constructive criticism and assistance to other seekers wishing to improve on those aptitudes that you've been practicing and applying from your positive list. This comes without condemnation or flaunting because you recognize that you've been there, done that. Having gone through the process makes us more sensitive to those who are still processing, and therefore better able to help them with loving intent as a foundation.

Refining Fires

A prayerful examination of one's life and ideals often leads to very perplexing questions. Why do bad things happen to me when my intentions are good? Why does it seem like I'm getting nowhere spiritually even with consistent effort? What gives? No one ever said that walking a positive spiritual path would be easy. Likewise, neither magick nor prayer has ever, nor will it ever, fix every problem in life. If anything, the first few brave steps down the road toward enlightenment are very unsteady and can be met with numerous personal, familial, and societal challenges. Rarely does one get comfortable (comfort leads to sloppy or lazy spirituality). Rather, as we become more confident and adept, we build that relationship with God/dess on all levels and reflect the strength of that relationship in how we "walk the talk." Those who come to Wicca or Neo-Paganism thinking it to be a quick-repair kit for life, or those who want drive-through enlightenment by practicing magick are in for a rude surprise.

Your life is your own. What you do with it—for boon or bane—is between you and spirit. Yes, there are going to be times when life is hard. Everyone has those ups and downs. The key is to not get caught in the quagmire. Just keep moving with one eye on the horizon and God/dess, and the other on terra firma. There are also going to be times when it feels like you're getting nowhere. Typically, this is when a lot of internal transformation occurs— when you measure your faith and how it inspires you, when you ask the hard questions and determine to find the answers. That is viable and important work. Don't get so caught up in the seeming lack of flash and fanfare that you forget the whys of your religion or where you've come from. Something *is* happening. It may be slow or tiny, but remember that the God/dess is very patient. He/She isn't going anywhere. All things in their own time.

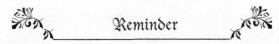

Reminder

Pray and meditate daily, extending your thoughts both outward and inward to feed that divine relationship and keep it growing in positive ways.

The Guru Trap

While relationship building and self-empowerment are wonderful, there is always the risk of the human ego running amok. In the process of reconnecting with the inner and outer God/dess, people sometimes stray. We hear what we most wish to hear and see what is comfortable or inspiring to ourselves or the group with whom we associate. This is a common problem. In the first case, we're looking for comfort and the satisfaction of feeling validated. In the second case, we're seeking acceptance. Unfortunately, both of these extremes can have devastating results.

By common definition, a guru is one who acts in spiritual *loco parentis* (in place of the parent or as a parental figure). When led by a true intense calling, such substitute parents can be amazing visionaries and guides to new ways of living. Flawed gurus, however, are a different matter.

The flawed guru exploits the concept of spiritual wisdom to feel powerful and gain control. A flawed guru can also be a truly caring individual who takes too much responsibility out of the hands of other people, thinking it's "for their own good." The guru feels wiser than the student and, therefore, believes he's better able to make choices (forgetting that the student is also God/dess, priest, guru, and guide for self).

Both types of flawed gurus lose sight of their own lives. They may have even felt overwhelmed by the complexities of life. Thus, they turn their attention outward to other "flawed" souls who are more than willing to hand over the reigns of control . . . they become "sheeple," or "sheep people." The sheeple believer then puts the flawed guru on a pedestal where he can continue to neatly avoid looking at his own personal issues—after all, the flock is what matters. This is a critical juncture in the guru syndrome. A person either gets out or turns into a cult leader, and we would hope that the former happens for obvious reasons.

Being a teacher, facilitator, or leader in any community comes with great joys and great responsibilities. As it is written, to whom much is given, much is expected. It can be very easy, very tempting, to slip over the fine line between helping and manipulation, between leading and ordering. If you keep the relationship between you and the divine healthy (within and without), and nurture it regularly, the chances of that happening lessen considerably. THOU ART GOD/DESS.

Commandment 2

The Judeo-Christian Second Commandment says, Thou shalt not make
unto thee any graven image, or any likeness of any thing that is in heaven
above, or that is in the earth beneath, or that is in the water under the
earth. Thou shalt not bow down thyself to them, nor serve them ...

———————•◦•◦•———————

Neo-Paganism teaches, As above, so below, as within, so without.

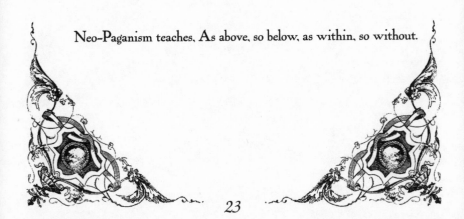

From high above the clouds, the world is one home. The ocean wraps around the earth as if to hold it in comforting arms. The darkness looks on casually from around the galaxies, its boundaries going on, and on. The Seeker cannot, as yet, fully comprehend this vast space especially when our own backyard still cries for understanding. What humans truly know—intimately and intuitively—of life's network is nearly as limited as our vision of eternity. So the quest turns to science, and faith, and an inquisitive spirit to fill the hungry mind and soul with insight.

Science showed us swirling molecules and swirling planetary systems. Our own eyes showed us starfish below the waters and the glorious stars above. And faith ... ah, the Spirit of Faith. This spirit has called to us again and again. It is yet another vastness, as far beyond us as we are above the atom. As children (albeit stubborn ones) of the universe, we try to hear and understand this call. Where is the Monad? It is within, but also without. It is in sounds and silences. It is in the in-between moments where nothing and everything coexist.

The Divine reaches out and leaves a fingerprint on its handiwork everywhere. That imprint waits: vibrating, ringing, singing of the Sacred Parent. As the Seeker wanders along the road, hints of that pattern emerge with both symmetry and chaos, as if to confound—when in fact, just the opposite is true. Balance is the answer, getting to the point is the answer, spinning the mandala in all directions until we rediscover center is the answer.

Along the road of life, one cannot become so consumed with the destination that they no longer internalize the journey. And one cannot keep looking at the path without loosing the horizon. Wisdom comes in realizing the difference.

As Above, so Below.
As Within, so Without

"As above, so below, as within, so without," speaks not only to one's relationship with self, others, the earth, and the cosmos but also their relationship with spirit. This creates an entire network of symmetry—sounds and silences, dark and light, the temporal and the eternal, a network of which we are an active part.

In distilled form, "as above, so below" means that we are god's vicegerent on earth, even as God is our master in the astral realm. This returns us to the reality of both internal and external deity we discussed in Chapter 1. Such a dynamic interconnectedness is the very thing that allows our will to act on the web of all things. Mind, body, spirit, and deity are all intertwined. When we connect with the divine through prayer, meditation, ritual, or any other line of communication, that union creates a direct line between the practitioner and the entirety of the universe and by extension the divine. The quality of that connection and our ability to master ourself determines how any particular working (the magickal/metaphysical process) manifests.

This creates a kind of natural push-me-pull-you within a spiritually aware person. There is a part of us connected to the earthly realm. This part is also imperfect and limited. Meanwhile our God-self and our spirit are linked to a wholly different realm where integrity, right intent, and perfected action are the ultimate goals. This conflict brings up natural questions like, "From what am I taking away, and what am I contributing to? What is the greatest good? Are we doing as much as we can based on what spirit asks of us? How can I honor my spirituality in all aspects of my life?"

Such questions lead to a place of humility, typically based on realizing the limits the body places upon us. Egos are an important facet of the whole human equation. However, when the higher and lower selves are trying to find symmetry, ego and arrogance typically do not help. Again, it's part of *know thyself.*

The spark of the divine within us yearns to be reunited with the divine without. It's normal for us, therefore, to seek out spiritual experiences. That quest, however, frequently gets derailed by our mundane responsibilities and the normal activities of day-to-day life. How many people can give several hours a week to worship, prayer, or meditation these days? More importantly, how do we fix that problem?

First, we must recognize that everything in this world has an astral presence. That dual presence means that your attitude toward any mundane task can turn it from ho-hum into something spiritually meaningful and magickally powerful. The key is recognizing potential in *all* its forms—from simple to sublime. It may be difficult to consider all the items around the house that you use regularly as having magickal potential, but consider it a playful challenge. Grab some paper and list a bunch of common objects like a toothbrush, batteries, buttons, a fork, etc. Then stop and think about how that item could symbolically and really be applied for a magickal goal. For example:

✝ **Toothbrush.** Since toothpaste is often mint flavored and mint is an herb associated with clear communications, why not use brushing your teeth as a means of cleaning up communications? Focus on that goal while you brush, then release any negativity when you rinse.

✝ **Batteries.** Batteries are all about the exchange of energy. You can use them as effective symbols for storing very specific types of power in amulets, talismans, etc.

✝ **Buttons.** What are you trying to hold in place or connect? Use buttons in spells. Or, as you button a piece of clothing, add little verbal charms as you fasten each button to provide the energies you most need/want.

✝ **Fork.** A fork is for piercing or holding. As you use a fork to cook or eat, think about those things that you want to keep firmly in place or illusions through which you want to see. Visualize that superimposed on your food so you can pierce through the darkness and find truth.

As you apply the concept of potential magick to more things in your life, you will also begin to surround yourself with positive spiritual energies and outlooks. Doing this becomes contagious. You'll be walking through the supermarket and a product name will resonate with something you've been pondering spiritually. Or you'll notice that a common household item suddenly takes on new meaning. When this happens, you should celebrate, as you're making spirituality a natural part of life. The here and now becomes filled with magickal potential that you can use regularly.

Black, White, Left, or Right?

The universe is our mirror. As we look into the world, something of self and the divine is reflected back to us. Where exactly do we fit in? What is the right or wrong way to walk our talk?

Physics tells us that energy is neutral. The application of energy, however, is not neutral. So humans, seeking definitions, start using terms like "good" and "bad," "black magick" and "white magick," and the "right-hand path" or the "left-hand path" to describe the results of applied energy and intention. Generally speaking, most practitioners define black magick as selfish, destructive, and manipulative. White magick, conversely, is giving, creative, and mindful of freewill.

Be aware, however, that black and white are only part of the spectrum. Left and right are only two directions or dimensions. These "extremes," if you will, are easier to see by the contrast they create and consequently attract our visual attention. But our eyes and souls are capable of seeing a myriad of colors, shades, hues, blends from gray to plaid! We are aware in everyday life of several directions: left, right, backward, forward, up, and down.

Additionally, the terms "black" and "white" do not necessarily properly describe the ethical component of a magus. In fact, historically speaking, "black" implied forcefully interacting with hostile or hazardous beings to try and engender their cooperation. Perhaps it's the forceful part that gave us modern folk the willies. After all, we talk about nonmanipulation.

We'd be hard pressed, however, to find all of the spirits that we encounter willing to help out those in the mortal realm. In fact, many spirits have agendas of their own. White magick was traditionally defined as dealing with those positive energies and beings active and present in nature (like devas), inviting the voluntary participation of such forces even as we continue to do with the watchtowers of the cardinal directions. Interestingly enough, there are no moral qualifiers here—just who the magus invoked. So if an herbal magus evoked a nature spirit to create a lustful potion, it was not considered immoral since nature spirits are neutral.

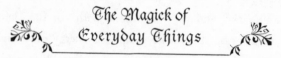

The Magick of Everyday Things

How can you improve the ways in which your spiritual life mixes and mingles with your mundane reality? Come up with at least twelve things that will do this work. If you're very busy, try adding one of those things into your daily ritual over a week or a month. That way, by the end of one year you'll have not only achieved twelve goals but also significantly changed your daily reality and made it more magickal.

Our notions of what traditionally constituted black, white, and gray were incorrect. The practitioners of ancient magick were not necessarily working on a specific ethical basis at all. What was once under the guise of "white" magick (like herbalism) is now being usurped by technology, science, and medicine. In many areas of daily life, we find ourselves turning to a reliable procedure and trusting in it, while we overlook the spiritual portion of the equation. For example, a dam might help direct a mighty river, but without putting a spiritual covenant in place with that river, the spirits of that place might break that dam. We can call our technology "good," and we can call our magick "white," but unless we honor all aspects of the equation to which we're applying our power, we will fall short and feel that lingering resonance (kind of like an itch you can't scratch).

Historical references aside, it would be naïve to say that evil does not exist. The law of balance requires that for there to be "good," there must also be the proverbial "bad." Today we say that a person who uses black magick or walks the left-hand path is considered to be working from a selfish or malevolent vantage point. In Lewis Spence's *Encyclopedia of the Occult* we read:

> To gain limitless power of god, demon, and man; for personal aggrandizement and glorification; to cheat, trick and mock; to gratify base appetites; to aid religious jealousies and bigotries; to satisfy public and private enmities; to further political intrigue; to encompass disease, calamity and death—these were the ends and aims of black magic.

For a person to exhibit this type of behavior externally in any realm of life, he or she would have to have that darkness as part of their makeup (the within) according to this concept. However, the question remains as to what is truly "black" and what's required necessary to raise that kind of energy. Some practitioners, for example, categorize working with entropy (the tendency of an energy system toward inertness through the breakdown of organized structure and pattern) or chaos energies as "black."

It receives this designation because, superficially, this so-called magick has the opposite effect from white (destroying or decreasing instead of creating). Yet the forces of nature perform these same functions. This makes us ask: if a form of energy exists in nature, can we call it "black"? Nature's pattern is eat or be eaten, which can seem very cruel. But, again, it is only illustrating balance. Some "black" magicians would reply that they, too, are illustrating the law of nature in becoming the predator instead of the prey, or in being protectively proactive (doing everything possible mundanely and magickally to safeguard that which they hold dear).

Since we are also animals, humans exhibit similar instincts. Yet, somehow we expect that our reasoning nature will suddenly take that instinct and put it neatly away like some toy that we've outgrown when we work magick. I'm not sure that's a wholly reasonable expectation, let alone a truly healthy one. Instead, a holistic approach would be to balance helpful instincts with rational thought and spiritual guidance.

Let's take this one step further, out of nature and into the divine realms. In the world's mythologies, we see images of gods and goddesses that take revenge against those who harm their followers (or children). We also see gods and goddesses that destroy to create. Kali (the Hindu Creatrix/Destroyer) comes immediately to mind. If the external divine uses the energy of reversal or diminishing, can that truly be called "black," or is it merely the universe's checks and balances? These are not easy ethical questions to consider or answer, but an honest examination of two things may help us gain some perspective—namely, intent (the internal motivating source) and the situation (the externals).

Let's say someone chooses to cast spells aimed specifically at exacting revenge because their family had been targeted by a person or a group. This would be considered gray magick, because it is a situation when an ill has been done and has not been balanced.

Now, the sender may not enjoy the feeling of that magick. There's a natural lingering temptation to lash out with unbridled anger and lose all focus. However, if similar circumstances occurred again, many people would be hard pressed not to do likewise. We simply want to protect those we love. Also, it is possible that people would feel inaction on their part would dishonor a sense of inner sacredness, and that sometimes we are the hand of karma (just as anything in life's network might be).

This is where the lines of black and white get blurred. You're not alone in facing a struggle between personal and spiritual ethics, potential karmic repercussions, and the natural desire to act . . . to do something, anything, to return the situation to a more equitable equation. It's part of human nature. If you find yourself in such a place consider the following advice:

‡ **Always step back and cool off.** Any magickal working is going to go better when you're thinking clearly.

‡ **Ask yourself if there is a mundane alternative that could fix things.** You can often use the energy generated by a bad situation to turn things around in your favor.

‡ **Always make sure you know (beyond any doubt) the focus of the spell.** Otherwise you could harm an innocent person.

✝ **Consider using a "universal clause"** (like "for the greatest good" or "and it harm none") so that no one on the edges of the situation gets harmed by the energy you're creating.

✝ **Pattern your response to only visit like for like** (no embellishing—think *balance*).

✝ **Continue personal efforts on the mundane level to rectify things and put your life in order.** This gives the universe more opportunities to open doors, heal wounds, and provide closure.

For a good book that discusses this subject in more detail than this book's space allows, try *How to Be a Wicked Witch*. Let's talk a bit about action and inaction and situational ethics.

Color Me Magickal

What color do you envision your magick being? Don't limit yourself to thinking in black and white. Does this color ever change? What do you feel that color (or colors) symbolize?

When You Mess Up—Clean up: Action, Inaction, and Consequences

There is a saying that goes, *karma simply is*. Karma is not an external force that imposes justice; it is a system of checks and balances that has no particular time frame. Karma also has no agenda other than illustrating the principles of cause and effect, action and reaction, total cosmic justice, and personal responsibility.

It is as impersonal as physics. It is the universe's way of balancing itself out in any direction.

There are several types of karma. The first comes from all actions in previous lifetimes. Think of this like a cosmic debt or bonus that you add to, or take away from, based upon your daily behavior. The second type of karma is from actions in this life. Third is what might be called "instant" karma, things that manifest daily, such as a person getting arrested for breaking the law. In this last example, we can see where karma's lessons come through experience; linking our action or inaction with *results* and *responsibility*.

Returning to my previous example regarding using magick for personal gain or revenge, karma asks questions like the following:

‡ Can you live with your choice? Can you look in the mirror and be comfortable with what you see?

‡ What kind of person do you wish to be?

‡ Are you ready to accept the responsibility for what you're doing, plus all possible repercussions?

These are three good questions to ask any time you're feeling uncertain about your motivations, and how best to proceed. However, in talking about action, inaction, and consequences, I think there are several other points to consider:

Sometimes life simply happens. Say you're in an accident and someone dies, but you live. Unless you purposefully and willfully had some hand in creating that accident, or in speeding that person's death, there's no karma involved for your current incarnation. In fact, there was very likely no karma involved in the accident. Death is a natural outcome of living! I only mention this because all too often people look for deep, spiritual meanings to things that have none.

There are many situations in which we do have some level of responsibility. In that case, it's time to take steps to ameliorate the damage. Being "sorry" is not enough. Apologies do nothing to fix things, other than perhaps making the person who did wrong feel a little less badly about it. Until we're ready to act on those things for which we're responsible, we have learned nothing. It's comparable to a child who continually engages in bad behavior because he or she thinks that mom and dad will either (a) give them positive or negative attention for it, and/or (b) forgive them. When they're old enough to understand the consequences of their actions, kids need to know better. They mess up, they clean up. This is a philosophy that applies very nicely to Wiccan situational ethics. If you've messed up, fix it to the best of your ability.

There are going to be some things you cannot fix. Say you initiate a huge fight with a family member. Afterward, you do everything in your power to seek out forgiveness and improve communications. If that person rebuffs your efforts, the karma is no longer yours to bear. Leave the door open and move on, knowing you've diligently and honestly sought peaceful closure.

Despite the power of magick, there are many things for which one must work physically, mentally, emotionally, and spiritually to remain as a cocreator with the divine. Within the broad Neo-Pagan community, there seems to be a creeping sense of entitlement. People expect magick to move mountains even when they've invested very little personal effort. For example, the creator of a ritual strongly suggests beginning at sunrise for the greatest amount of success. Well, to heck with that! We want to sleep until noon. Is it any wonder that such a ritual would go awry? While not all rituals require strict timing, in this illustration a timing was strongly advised. Without proper intent and honest effort, there's no reason for manifestation to happen. There was no real energy invested to begin with. The old saying, "There's no such thing as a free lunch" applies to magick, too. Be ready and willing to work for magickal manifestation.

Finally, what about those moments when our back is, indeed, up against a wall? A soldier will tell you that when shooting is about to start, you do something. This isn't the time for indecision. Such hesitancy on a regular basis creates the victim mentality in which you will remain on the sidelines of life as a proverbial wallflower. Yes, it's possible to make people angry through action. It's possible to do the wrong thing for the right reason, but to constantly do nothing isn't the perfect answer either.

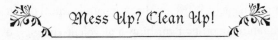

Mess Up? Clean Up!

The mage recognizes that for every action there will be an equal and opposite reaction somewhere. That's a law of physics over which we have no control. So watch the sky overhead, the ground under your feet ... monitor the illusions through which you're trying to move, and keep moving. When things happen because of your actions, take responsibility (not just in magick, but in life).

Be aware that *everything has consequences*, from taking out a loan or getting married to making tonight's dinner (or not). Well-crafted metaphysical methods define limits in some way to balance potential consequences. The boundary of our magickal constructs may be a person, an effect, a means to achieve the end, or the time at which the effect dissipates. Additionally, the wise witch is careful to restrict, deflect, and dispel potential contrary reactions that could harm herself or innocent bystanders. At the end of the day, even with precautions something can go wrong. Messed up? Don't wring your hands and say "poor me." Get up, dust yourself off, clean up, learn everything you can from the experience, and fix it.

Binding and Loosing Banishing and Invoking

When Neo-Pagans discuss action and inaction, the subjects of binding, loosing, banishing, and invoking typically arise. For example, should one worry about the karmic consequences of placing a binding spell on a harmful person or situation? Should we instead use protection spells, prayers, or rituals? And what about high magick? What are the moral and ethical implications of commanding spirits, banishing malevolent energies, or even drawing down a deity?

Think of binding as like putting handcuffs on someone or something. Similarly, banishing equates to not simply restricting but willfully carting someone or something away without their consent. There are times when both are perfectly appropriate spiritual reactions to a problem or situation, but I think we should keep those definitions in mind, as well as potential consequences that may occur.

Binding

The first question someone will inevitably ask himself or herself is, "Is it ethical to bind another person?" This seems to go against the basic code of nonmanipulation. Nonetheless, we speak of binding our hearts and hands together in a handfasting, which is certainly a situation in which people have a choice. This is an excellent example of where creating positive "ties" (which are not intended as reins or symbols of ownership) is not only an age-old custom but also perfectly acceptable. The individual is not lost in such an agreement, but enhanced by it.

On the other hand, what about a binding intended to offset perceived harm? There are some individuals who will listen to no amount of reason. Instead of binding the individual in a case like this, you may want to create a reflective bubble around his or her aura. This keeps most of the unwanted emotions from projecting outward. Since it is a person's choice to continue to act negatively, ultimately it's his or her karma that will be affected. The bubble itself has no other function and remains neutral until called into action by his actions.

Then, too, what about when binding seems to be for a person's own good, such as when a person has been contemplating suicide? This is a tough issue to resolve because it brings to bear many factors. The one thing that's truly ours in this life is our body. That's part of the reason why piercing and tattooing are so popular; they reflect ownership and individuality. After the age of reason, it's questionable as to how much right we have to interfere. But even as I type that last sentence I can hear some mother, somewhere, saying "And if you were about to jump off a cliff, wouldn't you want someone to warn you or stop you?" Since I'm not standing on that cliff, I honestly don't know.

Certainly, there could be mitigating circumstances. A person could be clinically depressed, be suffering a chemical imbalance, have critical health issues, etc. These circumstances (if known), combined with what your higher self seems to be saying, should yield some perspective. There are options besides binding, like an intervention or suggesting that this person gets counseling, both of which seem ethically sound. Even then, however, you don't know if any action will push the person over the edge, so you consider binding that destructive trait. At the same time, consider the cause for the trait, which could be very long-lived indeed.

As mentioned previously, I'm not an advocate of standing idly by when it's obvious that something should be done, when our inner (anyone's—i.e., OUR) god-self is screaming for action. As with so many other things in this book, mundane efforts are a primary option. We keep our magickal energy in reserve as a support system or to guide our actions as perfectly as possible. When all else fails, whisper a prayer and put trust in the universe for the greatest good.

Loosing

Continuing with the above-below equation, we must also consider loosing—people, ideas, outmoded habits, etc. There are a lot of things that we tie ourselves to in life, such as in the handfasting ritual described above. When separation occurs, however, those ties don't automatically disappear. They continue to affect us and resonate with energy from the other person. This is a good example of when loosing the binds would be helpful. You don't let go of the lessons, or of anything positive the relationship brought, but you do release the lines of energy that have connected each-to-each through your aura. The longer you've been together, the more complex those ties become. It can take a while to gently clear them away.

However, some of the ties in our lives also help and protect us, at least for a while. Think of a child's ties to family. The family provides structure and guidance that are intended to be helpful in life. Are they sometimes manipulative? You bet! However, simply removing all ties and structure from a child would be even more harmful, barring extreme examples such as abuse. Further, there are times when removing ties from a person or situation could be likewise damaging, especially if you're unaware of the complete picture. So, again, you're left to fall back on that inner God/dess and let spirit and old-fashioned common sense lead you to a decision.

Banishing

Let's start our discussion of banishing with a common example. Person A had a difficult family situation that left him or her filled with residual conflicts. Person A seeks advice, and someone says, "Why not banish the past?" At first that sounds like a grand idea . . . grand until the realization hits that we cannot wipe out the experiences, people, and things that have made Person A who he is today without some serious repercussions.

To illustrate further, perhaps Person A is very compassionate toward others struggling with family issues and even has a ministry (formal or informal) built on that foundation. If the energies that created Person A's compassion are banished, what happens next? Could his sense of charity shrivel and die because the substructure that birthed it is now gone? The possibility certainly exists. In this case, I would recommend a healing spell instead of a banishing, something focused on helping Person A retain the best lessons and growth from that difficult time, and release the rest (release the burdens).

Now if you're just trying to banish a negative personal outlook, that's a whole different story. Combine that desire with affirmations, and maybe tape yourself regularly to learn as to when that specific concept triggers in your awareness. Also work your banishing cooperatively with mundane efforts. If you use this type of thought process when considering any form of banishing (i.e., how do you keep the energies in balance), you'll be far more successful.

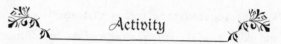

Activity

Come up with at least one example of a time in which you feel binding would be okay. After you have read the sections that follow, do the same exercise with loosing, banishing, and invoking. Reread your answers once a year to see how your perspectives have changed. This will show how you're growing and changing.

Both of these hypothetical situations were aimed toward ourself. What about the ethics of banishing a person from your life (because of abuse, illegal activities, etc.)? If all other efforts have failed, taking this step is reasonable, but not without considering how the absence of that person from your life may affect other people and situations in your life. We cannot be wholly aware of how one person's life-network might vibrate now or in the future. If you take this step, it might best be done using God/ddess as a copilot for the spell or ritual's energies.

Invoking

If there are potential ethical issues with banishing, invoking carries similar questions. How right and proper, in the greater scheme of things, is it for us to invoke spirits or aspects of the divine? One would think that gods and/or goddesses would have better things to do than come at our beckoning. And depending on the type of spirit we invoke, beings who live in other realms can have agendas of their own, some of which are probably not in our best interest, and others that cannot be understood completely by mortal minds.

When it comes to gods, goddesses, or the elemental powers, perhaps the word "invite" is better suited than "invoke." It is not necessarily ours to command such powers, unless it's our own god-self who speaks. The commonly accepted definition of "invoke"—"to earnestly request aid or protection; an appeal for help"—certainly allows for a less arrogant interpretation and seems respectful of the energies represented, with respect being a key element in the spiritual tripod completed by honor and gratitude.

When dealing with gods, goddesses, and other usually invisible entities, what the "correct" approach is often depends on the path we're walking. The high magician must show strength when dealing with certain beings. That is one of the reasons that this path is constructed with great attention to the details of each process and why any mage worth his or her robe stresses good training. Meanwhile, the folk witch rarely, if ever, has the need to "command" spirits. He or she might *commune* with the spirit of a plant or animal so as to use that energy more effectively, but invoking doesn't really play its hand.

To Know, to Will, to Dare, to Be Silent

This phrase wraps up the thoughts in this chapter nicely. How many of us really know all the spiritual tasks and lessons set before us? When we feel moved, what then is our will? What do we dare? When do we act, or wait . . . speak or remain silent?

My perspective on this statement follows.

To Know. With a calm, inner awareness we know that there is more meaning to life than what we can readily experience with our five senses, that there is more to the planet than water and land, and there is a great deal more to the universe than just human beings.

To Will. Our will is the way in which we move through this world. When each soul takes its evolution in hand and accepts responsibility for all actions and inactions, that is will, and it is a driving force.

To Dare. The fool leaps from the cliff—he or she dares to meet the challenge and learn to live. The path was never said to be easy. To reach your goals and put foundations under your dreams, dare to live up to your full potential as a God/dess.

To Be Silent. The art of listening is quickly being lost, not just listening to each other, but to the voice of reason, our own inner guidance, to the voice of the divine. Noise keeps us from facing the truths within and without. Silence transforms people and the world.

You will find that the last point is very powerful. Our world is filled with noise from without and within. The divine and the higher self must shout to be heard. When you seek after silence, suddenly that still small voice is clear, and you can begin to know it intimately.

3 Commandment

The Judeo-Christian Third Commandment says, Thou shalt not take the name of the Lord thy God in vain . . .

Neo-Pagans say, Spirit abides in all things.
Words and names have power.

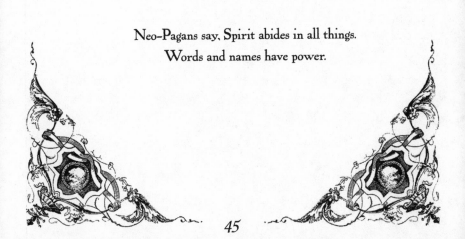

he Seeker discovers the unique, wondrous spark in all things; in the tiny insect, in the wind's breath, in the glowing morning sun, in the faces of children. This vision sets the Seeker's mind in a new direction—they begin to live differently, to BE differently. The awareness of one grows to an awareness of many . . . of the seen and unseen worlds where energies dance, play, and spiral the magick of the universe.

That energy is like a blueprint that was etched at the dawn of time, but not one of firm images or words. Rather, it is one built on amazing ideas that could not be limited. The Seeker engaging those ideas cannot help but transform . . . cannot help but live prayerfully . . . seeing and interacting with the blueprint of creation, and, more importantly, the architect.

As the pages of the blueprint slowly unfold and the Seeker begins to understand, he or she also wants that same sense of belonging for self—a name by which to be remembered; a name that resonates with all incarnations and the path itself. It is time to choose. It is time to find the power of Space and Name.

Spirit Abides in All Things. Names and Words Have Power

In Chapters 1 and 2, we pondered what it means to have the Great Spirit, within and without, above and below. Extending this idea, the next natural step is to see the pattern of spirit in creation itself. Most Neo-Pagans view the earth as a living, vital entity unto itself (or, as Gaia, herself). Whether or not we can call nature "intelligent" is subject to some fierce conjecture, but nature is certainly alive and certainly has a distinct order. Further, different regions of the world seem to contain energies specific to them, and it's nearly impossible to look at the wonders of the earth and not see the divine mechanism in motion.

Wiccans are typically Darwinian and environmentalist in their outlooks. While the divine got things moving initially, evolution is the built-in mechanism that allows for adaptation and change, including improvement. While humankind has done much to harm the planet, our reborn awareness is a good starting point for healing and rebuilding our relationship with nature. The ethical problem with this healing process becomes: When does our attempt to protect the land or its creatures actually make things worse? For example, controlled burns of forests are done periodically to try to preserve surrounding lands or trees. Yet, we know that in the process some part of the ecosystem will be lost to that burn. The answer to "burn or don't burn" is that we must trust whatever knowledge we have in that moment, and in the experts in a given field. I don't think we should stop asking questions or reevaluating how our environmental efforts are impacting things globally and long-term.

It is human hubris to see the earth as something over which we have dominance. Stand in the epicenter of an earthquake or a Category 5 hurricane and see how dominant you feel at that moment! This sobering reality, combined with our growing awareness of how deadly the human incursions into nature have been, has created a new movement toward stewardship. Stewardship has several aspects. Stewardship is:

- ✝ A cooperative venture in which we consciously recognize and reaffirm ourselves as part of the earth (as opposed to simply being "on" it, or having its resources at our disposal).

- ✝ An effort to understand all living things in their own terms rather than anthropomorphically, and then acting accordingly.

- ✝ Decreasing personal wastefulness and giving back from that which we use/take.

✝ Integrating mindful living in what we buy, consume, or use.

✝ A personal vow to begin rebuilding the earth in body, mind, and spirit for future generations. (Native American tradition says seven generations, but I'd challenge each awake and aware individual to look long and hard beyond even that. We've seen how even one generation can undo the good of several earlier generations.)

Now I know all this sounds lofty, but, sad to say, this list oversimplifies matters. There is so much that needs doing. The earth is a very big space that bears a lot of wounds. Where do we begin? What can we do that is for the good of all?

A key component to each individual's or group's successful stewardship may very well boil down to the injunction, *think globally and act locally.* The local part of the equation helps us create reasonable goals that relate to what *we're* doing and begin seeing viable results from those efforts, one step at a time. Without those results, it's easy to get discouraged and sink into apathy. There is nothing more destructive to the individual or the world than to stop trusting that one person can make a difference. It is also important for human beings to recognize all spaces as sacred, including the space of our own bodies, which leads us to the discussion of the power of place and how that changes our perspectives and affects our ethical outlooks.

Your Body Is a Temple: The Power of Place

Some places, whether through their ambiance, visual impact, or other sensory cues, embody the ideals of a person, culture, or faith. As individuals or groups discovered such places, they called them holy and acted more reverently there than in other places. But from a Neo-Pagan perspective every place is sacred. That little plot of grass outside an apartment, the tree at the corner, the weed in your lawn, the mosquito bothering you at night . . . everything is sacred, including you.

In Chapter 1, we pondered what Thou Art God/dess means personally and spiritually. That study cannot be left behind when talking about the power of place, because you, too, are a place—a bodily space that is wholly holy. Obviously, this doesn't mean the universe revolves around one person's body, but an awareness of personal sacredness helps us when we're trying to understand the concept of sacred spaces and places. In this case, your spirit or soul is the sacredness "within," and nature is the sacredness "without."

Consider:

‡ The Greek philosopher Porphyry spoke about trees having souls.

‡ Marban, a ninth-century Irish hermit, discovered God in the woods and in the company of birds.

‡ St. Anthony (300 A.D.) felt that nature was God's open book.

✝ St. Francis of Assisi (1181–1226) called all living things his brothers and sisters.

✝ St. Therese de Lisieux, a French Carmelite nun (1873–1897), taught that God was in all things and often spoke of "the book of Nature."

✝ Poet William Cullen Bryant (1794–1878) called the forests "God's first temples."

✝ In 1983 the World Council of Churches discussed the integrity of all creation.

✝ Fritjof Capra, Ph.D., said, "The whole universe appears as a dynamic web of inseparable energy patterns."

Consider for a moment what Ken Wilber wrote in *The Holographic Paradigm and Other Paradoxes*. He asserted that each breath we inhale has atoms that other humans have likewise breathed in the last two weeks (a quadrillion atoms to be exact, give or take a few). That's a pretty intimate connection and network.

Go outside, look around, breathe deeply, and think about the intimacy of that connection. The web of life has just become intimate—it's at your fingertips, under your feet, before your eyes, in reach of your ears, and in each breath you take. The pulse of the divine is no further away than our skin. It is *we* who separate ourselves from Nature and God, not the other way around. The true power of place starts to become a vital thing in our lives the minute we begin to truly recognize it and work toward undoing that separation, starting with the sacred self, every moment of every day.

The sacred, like God/dess, speaks to us in imagery to which we readily relate, and also through symbols that have meaning to us. The problem for most people is that we are too busy with other "important" matters to notice those glorious flashes of insight when they arrive at a mundane moment. To share a personal example, like most people, I don't think of my day job as being even remotely sacred. It's hard to feel divine when serving coffee (although someone enjoying the coffee might beg to differ). The other morning, however, a woman remarked about my hourglass tattoo, saying she thought it was a good reminder to live in the present. I was floored! Here I was cleaning up some spilled milk and sugar, and this spark of sacredness landed neatly in front of me with a profound message (one, by the way, that wasn't originally part of the reason for the tattoo).

This is an example of what I call spontaneous sacredness evoking the power of place, and it brings up the ethical question of, "what next?" It would be inappropriate to set up a shrine at work, no matter how meaningful that exchange was for me. It would be likewise inappropriate to lavish undo attention on this young woman, who wouldn't understand what the fuss was all about; for all I know, to her it was a casual conversation that may not have affected her at all. Nonetheless, if I honor that memory in the way I live, I likewise honor the sacredness, with or without an altar, except for the sacred space/place of self.

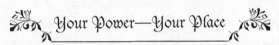

Your Power—Your Place

Ponder your personal power of place—that sense of self within your body. How do you feel as that "place" mixes, mingles with, and/or affects other sacred spaces?

It's pretty easy to see how the phrase "your body is a temple" takes on a slightly different vibration when you're talking about personal power and place. While it's wonderful to be able to go to a spot that really brings deity "home" emotionally, we often forget that deity is already home. Thou Art God/dess (God/dess is both within and without—we are spiritual beings).

Spiritual Centers

Moving from within to without, the awakened and aware spirit is one that will become a trailblazer in this realm and others. To fulfill that role, the seeker accepts and activates the role of the divine (Thou Art God/dess), lives in balance (as within, so without), and now takes the step toward remembering and rebuilding his or her connection with the ancestors, the tribe, the world, and, by extension, the cosmos. Our ancestors give us the gift of tradition and the tribe reminds us of our humanness—our needs, wants, goals, things of which the communal necessity of companionship and a supportive group of intertwined individuals cannot be denied. Finally, the earth becomes our teacher, our provider, and a reflection of the universe and God, and it has a few surprises in store for us along the way.

Children often sing to trees, guppies, and other elements of nature. In observing my own young children they don't seem to understand the idea of sacredness in adult terms, but they know there's something special in nature—these are certainly holy interactions filled with innocence and being. It seems unlikely that as adults we can each reclaim that sense of place and space.

I was walking to work one day when a bird landed near my feet and sang a little tune. Without even thinking I replied, "Good morning to you, too." Now this wouldn't have been odd in the least until I realized moments later that I had not heard the bird saying, "Chirp, chirp, chirp." I had quite clearly heard, "Good morning." More interesting still was that it felt as natural as breathing to listen that way. In that moment, I had found my power of place. Now, I do not believe that sidewalk was a spiritual center. This was a one-time instance and I've never noticed anything out of the ordinary there before or since, but the experience changed forever the way I think about nature.

True spiritual awareness means being present and paying attention. It means finding the power of your personal space, so that other spaces (teaching spaces, praying spaces, ritual spaces, be-ing spaces) make themselves known to you. Even a concrete slab can house sacred energies. Walls can talk but people don't always listen. If you're already living in the moment, and listening to your inner/outer God/dess, you'll probably find special sanctuaries quite naturally, as children often do without realizing it. As an adult, however, it helps to have some guidelines as to what type of sensations to look for when you stumble upon a sacred place. These cues include:

‡ A tingling sensation (like static)

‡ The feeling that you've stepped into another time or dimension (due to a shift in energies)

‡ A sudden hush or calm around and within

✝ Intense emotional, physical, creative, or spiritual responses to a place or space evoked without warning

✝ Unusually lush plant or animal life

✝ The presence of light (or brighter light) as compared to adjacent areas

Unlike spontaneous sacredness, many spiritual centers have long-term, regionally specific holiness that's often recognized by a wide variety of people, some of whom may not be spiritually oriented. Many people believe that these centers take their resonance from a historical event, from ley lines, from a unique composition of plant matter or stones, etc. In any case, whatever exists in that spot makes people feel differently—more awake and aware. And once such a place is discovered, the next obvious question is what do we do with this awareness, this powerful place? What is our ethical responsibility?

The most common responses to that question are "protect them, of course" and "bring other people here to experience this." If we see the earth as sacred, this place isn't really *more* sacred, it just affects *us* differently. Does that one spot deserve our extra protection, versus those efforts we extend on a planetary level? If we're thinking globally and acting locally, perhaps the best thing is to devote our energy to safeguarding that spot, knowing that by extension it ties into the greater all. But shouldn't we ask the spirits of the land first? What do they want?

It is not our place to trample into nature, add magickal energy willy-nilly, and walk away feeling puffed up and pleased with ourselves. To honor the earth, it would be nice to make an effort toward a polite introduction, reconnection, and relationship-building process with nature. It respects the power of place. The change in attitude turns a personal expression into a sacred excursion.

And how does bringing other people to sacred spaces figure into relationship building and respect? It depends on how you look at it. Many people would rejoice in revealing such energies to another being and watching the wonder in their exploration. However, would we be doing this for their good or because of personal desire? It's similar to a child saying, "Look what I found!" It's natural to want to share, but we must always consider the other seeker's best interest. Would it be better for them to discover the power of place in their own time? Or would experiencing it communally be even a greater expression of the indwelling wonder and divinity of all things?

Do or don't do. Those are really the options. Either decision, however, should be guided by the God/dess, tempered by balance, and nurtured by positive intention.

Mindful Living

It would be remiss to discuss the power of place and living in balance with the earth without discussing the concept of mindfulness. Most people think of mindfulness as being sensitive to all creatures and environments in body, mind, and spirit, but that's really only one small fragment of this philosophy. If you think about this word as a compound term (mind-fullness), the idea becomes a little easier to grasp.

Begin with the mind half of the term. It's our vehicle for thought. It helps us interact with and understand our entire reality. That mind is continually busy processing all manner of impulses—everything from interpreting what our eyes see and hands feel to the tidbit of conversation overhead on the street. These are like files that fill the cabinet of the mind.

Now, if those everyday times weren't enough, there are all kinds of other input. With what proverbial paperwork do we fill our minds (positives, negatives, should-bes, never-was, etc.)? How do we still such thoughts that undermine the sacred self and learn to cultivate the mind of perfect love, truth, reality, and awareness that stimulate enlightenment? How do we extend that mindfulness in true balance (within and without) so that it becomes naturally reflected in our ethics?

Practicing mindfulness isn't something that comes easy, especially in Western society where multitasking has become an art. However, I truly believe that once we begin living mindfully, a great many other aspects of our faith and philosophy naturally fall into place. Here are some tips to get you started:

> **Don't rush the rituals of life; savor them.** No matter what they are, allowing stress and distractions into those rituals is part of what causes imbalance. The rituals of our lives provide comfort and a sense of structure into which we can then pour our bodies, minds, and spirits to fill things out successfully. Go a little more slowly and watch your life change.

> **Don't give in to social pretext.** For example, if you ask someone, "How are you?" you should really want to know, not simply speak polite words. In this case, be ready to listen and honestly respond to what that person is saying. Or when you meet someone for the first time, don't allow your socially conditioned self to jump to judgment. Allow that person's power of place to unfold naturally rather than basing your

reactions on a similarity to other people with whom you've had positive or negative interactions.

This "allowing" goes for regions too. Let the energies of the earth make themselves known. Forcing feelings and relationship causes undue stress. Here are some helps and hints that begin to make living mindful and allowing something more natural and comfortable:

- ‡ **Breathe.** A good spiritual vitamin to take is simply stopping for a few seconds, and breathing deeply. Find your center of balance, your power.

- ‡ **Find a hobby that can help keep you in touch with nature, even if indirectly.** A potted plant on a windowsill is still part of nature. The spirit of the plant can become a valuable teacher.

- ‡ **Release yourself from technology on a regular basis.** Turn off the TV and your computer and find time for quiet and stillness. Mindfulness is very difficult to achieve when our minds are already filled with noise.

- ‡ **BE.** Take time to nurture your relationship with your inner God/dess and get to know that aspect of yourself more intimately.

Language studies can also be helpful in understanding mindfulness a little better. In Sanskrit, the word for "mindful" means "remember," while in Chinese the ideograph means "present heart." Put those two together and you get a rather intense approach to living here and now. We are still mindful of the past and remember things that created our present, but our mind is tuned to this moment, now, to the potentials and powers of this moment, and how to make it really count. Now is the time to begin retraining your mind to focus, find solutions, and then put those answers into effective, moral action.

Mindfulness in Motion

Name three ways to begin applying mindfulness in your daily life. (For example, make a daily list of items you can recycle at work, and make that a goal.) Learn to set reasonable goals. Prioritize them and start living them. Start retraining yourself to deal with problems instead of avoiding them. Make a commitment to yourself, your environment, and the people in your life. Commit to being positive and contributing to worthwhile causes. Dare to dream, then work to make your dreams come true. Build on your commitment by focusing on what's really important.

The Power of Names and Words

Words create images in our minds. A name may create a mental image and a feeling. However, we're often unaware of just how intensely names and words affect our daily reality, let alone our spirituality.

Names

Once we own our places and power, it's not surprising to discover that the idea of naming comes into the picture. A name defines a person or place. It gives it a unique point on the universal map. Names provide identity, they can identify associations, strengths, and weaknesses. They affect the power of place by those attributes. It is no wonder that a great deal of superstition and folklore surrounds the giving and changing of names.

From an ethical and philosophical perspective, we must consider various things when talking about the power of naming. First, most magickal practitioners choose a new name for themselves at least once in their lifetimes, as well as special names for covensteads, sacred sites, etc. These names need not follow social convention, but they do need to follow spiritual leadings.

From a mundane perspective the question would arise: why choose a new name? Meanwhile, spirit asks, why not? When we are born, our family gives us a name that's meaningful or pleasing to them. When we become spiritually active adults, that name may no longer really "fit" who and what we've become. Thus, we choose a name that is more reflective of who we are and all that we hope to become.

Let's face it, the Neo-Pagan community has hundreds of Merlins, Bridgits, Sunshines, and Moonbeams running around. While those might have been lovely names at some time in history (the sixties come to mind), and while the names may be very meaningful, there's something about them that may turn people off, both within and without our community. Our society (the without) has, for the most part, remained relatively conventional in its naming protocols. So when these individualistically minded pagan folk start introducing themselves with names that sound like they come from The *Lord of the Rings* or *Dances with Wolves*, people naturally wonder about that individual's sincerity along with the validity of the path they represent. It's just too "out there" for most limited thinkers.

No, you should not give up the name to which you felt called spiritually. That would not honor your inner God/dess. However, as a potential representative of the Wiccan and Neo-Pagan community, you do have an ethical responsibility to present yourself professionally in the outside world. So either use your legal name or find an alternative normal-sounding pseudonym that you can use when dealing with people who simply don't understand the visionary aspect of our path. This is not only considerate of their "space," but it also reflects positively on our community as a whole. Respect is a two-way street, and sometimes it means making people more comfortable so that they can listen without prejudgment.

Three other considerations in choosing and using names are changing social awareness, cultural meaningfulness, and (most important) what energies the name evokes. For example, at one time the word "squaw" was used as part of place names without a second thought (Squaw Peak in Phoenix, Arizona, for example). However, now that we know that the word refers to the female genitalia, we have all but eliminated it from use because it's not politically correct. Likewise, from a cultural perspective, a person may love the way a name sounds, but upon further research he or she discovers negative connotations (like naming a pet Loki, and discovering the mischief that god embodied). Remember that once something gets named, everything associated with a name goes along with that word. You can't just take one part and leave the rest behind. Please keep those things in mind any time you're choosing a new name for yourself, a group, or even a place (like your house).

The Word, the Pen, the Sword: Think, Speak, Write, and Weave Magick with Clear Understanding

Talking about names naturally leads to pondering how much power the written and spoken words bear, with or without our willfully intending them to do so. Anyone who sends e-mail on the Internet understands that power all too well. You wrote a message and intended one thing, but the person receiving the e-mail read a completely different meaning. This typical experience illustrates the power of words. Their power is not simply in the mind of the writer or speaker, but also in the mind of the reader or listener. What happens, then, when a linguistic disconnect occurs between what's written in a book and what happens in the context of ritual space? Say a person enacts a companion spell. They do not wish to manipulate, so they simply put forward the basic personality desired in a companion. They could end up with a "friend," a life mate, or a really wonderful dog. Yikes!

As the aphorism rightly says, "The pen is mightier than the sword." Our ancestors were aware of the truth of word power. In magick and life, they chose their words carefully. Whole languages developed around key issues in a representative culture, and the feelings of that people toward those issues. Additionally, stories from around the world illustrate a strong belief in the power of words. Consider:

‡ In the Bible, God speaks all things into existence.

‡ The Egyptian god Ptah utters words of manifestation to begin the universe (and Egyptians called their written language the speech of the gods).

‡ In Greco-Egyptian magical papyri, the names of non-Greek and non-Egyptian deities are invoked, as well as long strings of vowel sounds. Historians feel these may have served a purpose similar to the Indian mantra, namely to transport the chanter into an extraordinary state of being or to impart power and energy to the magickal spell or ritual.

‡ Samurai warriors used a *kiai* (shout of power) to focus themselves and direct their intention before battle.

‡ The bard or troubadour of the Middle Ages used the emotional power of words (in song and poetry) to sway people either to help with a political or social cause, or to increase the amount of money received for a performance.

The problem with talking is that we're not always speaking the same language. For example, when you think of a charm what comes to mind? A token on a bracelet? A little item you carry around to invoke magickal results? A verbal spell with a song like quality? All three of these responses are correct, but only the last one is historically accurate. Charms began as nothing more than verbalized, willful wishes (often rhymed) that directed energy. It wasn't until much later in history that objects were considered or called charms (when, in fact, they should have been more accurately considered amulets or talismans). This is a good example of how language use changed, and as it did the power of the word likewise transformed.

Let's take another illustration that's been getting lots of media coverage. The use of the word "Christmas" for the winter holiday has been hugely debated in the public and private sector because it singles out one faith. Most Neo-Pagans celebrate Yule or Winter Solstice. Jews have Hanukkah. Using the accurate term for a celebration clarifies many things and prevents misrepresentation. Even so, I still often find myself slipping into calling the holiday season "Christmas," as it is typically referred to on store speakers, in media ads, etc. Does it hurt anything to call it Christmas? In a very small way, perhaps yes. That is not what's being celebrated in my home. There is energy in the words "Christmas" and "Yule," and honoring word power means that the words we use should honor the meanings of those words.

There are some helps and hints that can help us with the goal of changing our communications so they ethically and conceptually reflect our true intent. First, remember that thoughts are words spoken in our minds and are thus just as important as verbalizations spoken aloud in terms of how they affect our psyche. The words we use to think and speak about something can and will, over time, transform the way we think about that something. Similarly, if we work on thinking about something differently, we'll begin to talk about it differently. This also illustrates the lesson of Chapter 2, as above (thought), so below (speech or written word); as within (thought), so without (speech or written word).

One of the best exercises to put this concept into action is to choose one spiritual aspect of yourself that you'd like to change. Each time you bring up the objective toward which you want to work, speak of it as you would an accomplished goal. Affirmations help with an activity like this. For example, if you're not terribly tolerant of novice practitioners, add an affirming chant to your next jogging or walking session, repeating to yourself: *I am patient*. Similarly, each time you think about the unwanted quality you're releasing, also think about it as a "done deal." Working this way, within and without, will eventually transform behavior to mirror your thoughts and words.

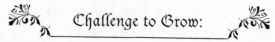

Challenge to Grow:

Challenge yourself daily to grow, inwardly and outwardly. Learn from the past, but don't cling to it in your thoughts or words. Be brave. Try new things that motivate you to use more positive thoughts and words. Ask questions, listen to answers, then integrate your lessons so that they too can be reflected in your future thoughts and words.

An effective speaker is an adept listener—begin by listening to yourself. What words and phrases do you use regularly about yourself or others? How do these hurt or heal? Now, pay attention to how those around you communicate to each other (especially to children). Watch how helpful words rebuild the sacred self, whereas harmful ones come across almost like a physical slap.

Abusive or manipulative language is the sign of an abusive or manipulative personality. A gentle voice typically reflects a gentle spirit. Don't just "hear" words. Extend all your senses to your modes of speech and those of others. How do your words taste? How do they feel in your gut? If you can answer that honestly, you can tell how they'll feel to someone else.

The main limits to success are those we create in our thoughts and words. The best advice I've heard on this matter comes from Don Waterhawk, coauthor of *Sacred Beat*, who instructs us to insert the word "trust" where we would normally say "hope" or "wish." Trust implies something firmer: it carries the power of faith.

Language is often accompanied by a visual component to improve communication. Consider how often people jump to the wrong conclusion during a telephone conversation because they see no body language to help them interpret the speaker's intention. We depend on more than one sense in using and conveying word power.

Magickally, one of the most well-known examples of matching visual cues to the goal comes to us from the Gnostic charm *Abracadabra*, which is commonly written in a slowly diminishing triangle. This visual effect is exactly what the word means (to perish like the word, something often used in banishing disease or sickness). Combining spoken and written language creates a symbiosis whose power increases geometrically. Think of it this way:

1. I write a poem with meaning X in mind.

2. Person A reads the poem and finds a completely different level of meaning (or unanticipated variations in my original meaning).

3. Person B reads the poem out loud and he or she (along with each person listening) finds yet other meanings.

This one bit of word-power has grown in its ability to affect others because of human uniqueness, and how each of us interprets what we read and hear.

Sound is vibration. How we perceive it or use it depends on the delivery of the tones and their relationships to each other. So it isn't simply *what* you say, but *how* you say it. I would actually take this concept one step further in that the recipient's way of listening (their personal "space") may change the way those words are received, no matter what your original intention is. It reminds me of the powerful quotation by Robert McCloskey, "I know that you believe you understand what you think I said, but I'm are not sure you realize that what you heard is not what I meant." Such things happen all too often when we have no point of reference through which to interpret or convey our words, such as in e-mail.

Different rhythms and sounds are capable of arousing different sensations and emotions in humans. When we rock children at night, our voices take on a sing-song tone for a valid psychological reason. Similarly, when working toward personal or community transformation the rhythm and tone of our communications must, of needs, reflect those goals.

If you have a word for it, you can think about it, and if you can think about it you can begin to manifest it at least on a personal level. However, in that process consider grammar, word order, and popular expressions. The relationships between words reflect the relationships within a culture of humans to each other, humans to their society, as well as humans to the world around them. This relationship doesn't change when we talk about magick, spirituality, ethics, and philosophy.

Meaning is everything. To some, the word *abracadabra* could have a great effect, especially to someone who knows its historical roots, or when it is spoken to a superstitious group theatrically by someone they respect. The word *abracadabra* has no meaning by itself, however. This is a very clear example of the importance of knowing your "audience."

The Law of Pragmatism simply states, "If it works, it's true." And I wouldn't hesitate to add here, "If it ain't broke, don't fix it." Sometimes we get caught up in the "fancier is better" mode of thinking, even in how we communicate. If you have never thought about this, just look at greeting cards—too many flowery words, too little true meaning, and often no real message.

Words generate information, store it, transform it, or perform some combination of the three. In so doing, they impact our individual and collective awareness. This is another good reason to choose words carefully, thoughtfully, mindfully, and responsibly. How do you want to change your world? Then talk about it accordingly.

Each language has its own power of place. Therefore, avoid using languages with which you're not intimately familiar for important communications or for magickal workings. Slight changes in inflection can impact clarity and comprehensibility quite easily. While the other possible languages might sound very exotic and magickal, what results from using them is likely anything but exotic.

Thinking the Think

Last, but certainly not least, positive thinking and speaking changes the spirit. The biggest difference between humans is their attitudes.

> Most folks are about as happy as
> they make up their minds to be.
> —Abraham Lincoln

If you are what you think, and you are what you feel, now is a good time to ask yourself, "What do I think? What am I feeling? Where am I going, and how do I want to get there without straying from the Path of Beauty?" These aren't easy questions, and you're not going to answer them overnight, but it is important to eventually find some answers.

The attitudes and outlooks that you bring to Neo-Paganism are the products of many factors, from your family, culture, and society to personal experience. However, now you have the opportunity to choose attitudes and outlooks that promote wholeness.

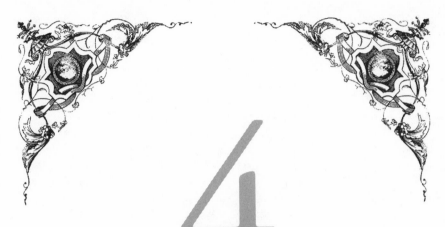

4 Commandment

The Judeo-Christian Fourth Commandment says, Remember the sabbath day, to keep it holy. Six days shalt thou labour, and do all thy work: but the seventh day is the sabbath of the Lord thy God: in it thou shalt not do any work . . . .

❖━━━━━━◆❖◆━━━━━━❖

Neo-Pagans teach, Maintain an Attitude of Gratitude (Walk the Talk).

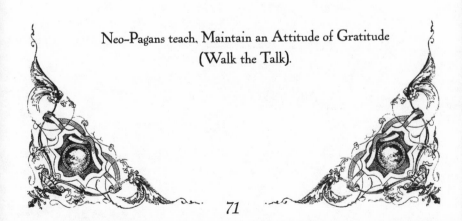

s the Seeker embraces the power of Name and Place, he or she begins to see things in a new way. The potentials of the universe unfold like a flower in all their unlimited loveliness. The Path of Beauty bears that name for a reason, but this is not a "human" beauty in trivial forms. It is an eternal beauty, a modest sacredness—a pattern of perfection that spans all people, all beings, all things, all places, all spaces, all times and reflects both creation and Creator.

A simple stone glistens with dew and sunlight. A flower turns to greet the sun. Streams and oceans flow unerringly to their destination, never wavering or worrying about the twists and turns along the way. The tree never questions where it stands. Meanwhile, Silence blesses a weary heart. A child giggles in innocent pleasure, becoming the twinkle in the God/dess's eyes. And life ... oh, my! Life sings with a joy and awareness that's indescribable. For this, and so much more, we give thanks.

Maintain an Attitude
of Gratitude
(Walk the Talk)

Perhaps one of the biggest gripes in the general magickal community is directed at people who "play" at spirituality and religion. Some come to festivals or circles to escape real life for a moment, but with no real spiritual intentions. Others use it as a social occasion where they like to "party" (despite the festival facilitators' concerned efforts to keep the tone of a gathering on the right track). Others still are seeking attention by doing something outside the mainstream. Call them party pagans or weekend warriors, the common thread among these individuals is that the initial reasons for being involved in metaphysics isn't necessarily for enlightenment or personal growth. Consequently, they often behave in ways that reflect poorly on the entire community.

By comparison, the serious witch and spiritual seeker live differently. For them, magick is a useful tool, but the philosophy and ethics for using that tool come from within. A Spanish saying states, "Tell me who you walk with, and I will tell you who you are." I'd go one step further to say, "Tell me where you walk, and what you do along the way, and I will know your spirit." The party pagans aren't really walking anywhere; they seem to have lost the roadmap.

As one grows and matures along a spiritual path, the hope would be that we would become more responsible. It's important to realize that we all started somewhere—and, yes, some of us started out as party pagans. But we can't measure the actions of a spiritual child by the same standards that we use for an adult. Children don't have the advantage of many years of life experience, learning, etc., that adults have. It's better to ask, what expectations do we put on each other at various stages along our spiritual path, and how reasonable are those expectations? How will our spiritual maturity (or lack thereof) be reflected in our ethics and philosophy? To what proverbial piper do our feet respond (and when and why)? How can we help those "playing at faith" find the more serious side of belief? These are core questions that persons of all faiths face at one time or another. Now is the time for our community to ponder them.

Walking the Talk (Your Daily Life Should Reflect Your Beliefs)

Speaking of party pagans, some paths start off badly from the get-go. The first thing that easily derails the goal of spiritual living is getting involved in any path with the wrong motivations, such as tweaking family or teachers (trying to get their attention) or because becoming a pagan seems like the trendy thing to do. Either situation leads to a very rocky road because the core motivation is wrong. This stumbling block in and of itself may not completely waylay a person's future success in a specific spiritual tradition (such as Dianic), but it will certainly present some challenges, a fair number of which won't be pleasant. There are very real consequences for ill-reasoned religious conversions. These come immediately to mind:

‡ The people around an individual will not trust him or her regarding future "convictions," meaning he's going to waste a lot of time and energy proving his sincerity.

‡ The individual's sense of self-trust will be undermined, consciously or subconsciously. Most people really do know when they're doing the wrong thing, or the right thing for the wrong reasons. Such knowledge affects the way you feel about yourself, if only in retrospect.

‡ People negatively affected by the pretender will draw pessimistic conclusions about Neo-Paganism that will affect their interactions with, and thoughts about, the entire community. It's often said that a lot of good people get judged wrongly (or suffer consequences) because of the bad behavior of a few. This holds very true here.

The way to turn around this misadventure isn't easy. The negative energy and karma certainly affect that person's aura and spirit, and it may take some time to be cleaned out. It's certainly not impossible to achieve, especially if that person learns from the mistake and fixes any damage they've caused in the process, but it seems much simpler to be honest with yourself (*know thyself*) from the start.

Another common reason that a seeker's path wanders into the woods is because of life's ups and downs. We get busy or distracted, and suddenly our spiritual life is placed on a shelf and left there to gather dust until the next coven meeting or Neo-Pagan festival. This is a situation we can avoid with a little creativity.

To stay on the path, stay aware that you're a spiritual being. Let that awareness simmer in your consciousness so that it seeps into your thoughts and actions. Find opportunities throughout the day that can have spiritual significance. Earlier, we talked about situational sacredness. That's the kind of energy you want to generate every moment. And while I will admit that mundane reality doesn't make that goal an easy one, it's more than worth our time and efforts.

Ritual and Routine

One thing that may help you maintain your spiritual awareness is to periodically assess your daily routine and schedule to see where you can nurture those all-important spiritual connections. Make a list of scenarios that occur with some regularity throughout your days. Next to your scenarios, write down something you could easily do that would invoke spiritual thoughts or actions. For example, in the morning, it only takes a moment or two to light a candle and welcome the divine into your home and day. Put the candle near your coffee cup or in the kitchen as a reminder. By intentionally lighting the morning candle regularly, with a specific meaning and purpose in mind, it becomes natural and ritualistic. On the way to work, listen to spiritually uplifting music that reflects your ideals and goals. Hum those tunes when you become frustrated or weary during the day. On the way home, voice affirmations that release the stress of the day, and balance your aura for the sacred space of home. When you clean, add blessed tinctures or other aromatics to the wash water to bless the whole home with intention and mindfulness. At no point in any of this have you gotten behind in your tasks or responsibilities. You have, in fact, made many of them more enjoyable because now you're multitasking on a different level—a level that meets the mundane and spiritual needs at the same time. Give it a try.

A third reason that it may become hard to walk a path stems from internal conflict, a contrast between what someone says versus what he does. If you don't walk the talk, you can't get where you're going. If your gait is impaired, so is your progress, and there's going to be some type of side effect. Perhaps you'll get completely off track and lose sight of your spiritual nature altogether. Perhaps you'll find yourself among people who are not healthy for your spiritual development. Perhaps others will question your sincerity. Maybe you'll just feel lost and confused. If any of these feelings or situations seem familiar, it may well be time to stop for a moment and reevaluate your path—not simply its direction, but also why you started walking it in the first place.

It has often been said that we cannot know where we're going until we consider where we've been. Look back, and see from where you've come and be thankful for that road. After all, it's your journey that has made you who you are today. Ask yourself what happened along the way that created obstacles, caused you to trip, or left you off balance. Knowing the persons, places, or things that are at the root of your spiritual stagnation is at least half the battle. Then, you can begin doing some serious weeding to clear the path and start making progress again.

I should note at this point that a spiritual path will rarely be completely free from problems. The difficulties in our lives are often the best teachers. No one can tell you the best pace for walking that path. You, as your life's guru and guide, must find the stride that makes for lasting and fulfilling changes, and adjust it according to circumstances. Most importantly, your "walk" must be one of internal and external integrity and gratitude. Without those qualities, there is no true movement.

Weighing the Wiccan Soul

Are there days in which you feel weighted down or as if you're getting nowhere fast? Join the club. All of us have baggage that we carry with us from the past—anger, resentment, or any number of issues that drag at our feet. We must remember that when we choose to "pick up" those issues. How we resolve them is also our choice.

Egyptian mythology tells us how Anubis, a god of the underworld, weighs the heart of each newly deceased person. The heart is placed on one pan of a scale, and Maat's feather of truth and judgment is laid in the other. If a person was wicked or dishonest in life, his heart outweighs the feather. His soul is fed to a crocodile demon called Ammit. This ended that person's presence forever with no possibility of future incarnations. On the other hand, Osiris welcomed the "lighter," more honorable souls into the Blessed Land.

This story leads me to wonder what would be the Wiccan or Pagan version of Maat's feather. Where is our spiritual scale? How much should our soul weigh?

In looking at the Neo-Pagan movement, it seems clear that more than one type of scale exists to measure our hearts. There's the scale of family opinion, the scale of personal experience, the scale of the influence of our culture, just to name three. This means that at any place along our path the weight of our soul can fluctuate.

The law of "as within, so without" dictates that the soul is like our body. It will be lighter or heavier depending on the way we exercise our spiritual nature, what we consume spiritually, the overall consistency of our protocol, and prevalent circumstances of our life. For example, if we weigh the soul of a person who just lost their temper, it's likely to be heavier than when that person is happy or thankful. But that extra weight is transitory. It's something we can fix.

Other weights aren't so easily resolved, like the pain that comes from a failing long-term relationship or a sudden loss of a loved one's life. These kinds of situations truly try our faith. We can hope that we've lived in such a way as to create an "ideal weight" for our soul to which it will always try to return with time, like elastic and certain foams that "remember" their shape. But, again, that can only happen if we're truly and consistently walking our talk with integrity. Then the pattern of sacredness becomes like a fingerprint in our spirit.

The principle of Maat's feather implies a kind of judgment. Maat's feather does not, however, get placed on the scale by another human being. It is impossible for one person to know with certainty—and without prejudice—the true disposition of another person's relationship with deity. A god-figure places the feather carefully next to your own heart. In other words, it's ultimately the sacred self that weighs your soul. That best, true part of you is kind of like Santa Claus in that it knows what's naughty and nice, and where the boundaries lie. Unfortunately, if a person hasn't developed a relationship with the inner God/dess, it's hard to hear that still small voice of reason and righteousness. And without that voice guiding us, it's no wonder our soul and spirit get weighted down with unhealthy and harmful things.

It is part of our human experience to go through a process in trying to weigh our soul. Elements of this process are:

✝ Not knowing for sure,

✝ Knowing but not listening,

✝ Listening but not understanding,

✝ Understanding but defying, and then eventually

✝ Coming around to understanding and acting on experiential awareness,

✝ Being thankful for the completion of the circle.

If you watch children at play, you will see all of these stages. Knowing is not enough—we have to be able to apply what we know. Understanding isn't enough because without action or transformation, understanding alone doesn't accomplish anything in the real world. For example, a person might "know" about what tsunami victims are experiencing at the time of this writing, but unless he or she acts on that knowledge thoughtfully and wisely, it's just a passing bit of data without any real power behind it. It will weigh down the soul because that person did, indeed, have that moment of enlightenment but chose to let it go by.

Maat Meditation

For the meditation, you'll need a feather (an ostrich feather is ideal but any natural feather will do). Sit comfortably in front of a mirror, holding the feather in your lap. A mirror can represent many things: the illusions of our life, our perspectives, but right now, we're pondering the mirror of the soul. So direct your gaze at your own eyes in the mirror. Look just beyond the surface of the mirror and let your eyes fall out of focus. Blink naturally and breathe deeply. Imagine a small flame appearing in your eyes. This is the heart flame, the light of the soul. Follow that light into yourself. As you move from outer reality to inner vision, feel free to close your eyes if you wish. When you find your visualization leads you close enough to touch your own flame, take it gently in your dominant hand. In your other hand, hold the feather. You are now Maat's scale. You are weighing the feather against your own essential being. Is it filled with *light*ness? Or are there things attached that weigh it down? If you see anything that's dark or blotchy in the flame, use the feather to flick it away. You don't need dark and blotchy things holding you back, nor do you need them changing the basic DNA of your spirit into something less than positive and sacred. Release the heaviness. Embrace the light.

After completing the Maat Meditation, write down how you see your own soul. Is it light or heavy? Is it old or young? How can you find ways to lighten (*enlighten*) your soul through daily activities?

Before moving forward, I'd like to add something here that I think is vital to your consideration of scales and measures. We are not perfect, and most of us are our own worst critics. What we would never condemn in someone else, we often find impossible to bear in ourselves. While holding high standards for the sacred self is a good thing, lofty expectations can end up causing more harm than good. Part of being human is being imperfect, and inevitably you will sometimes make mistakes. What demonstrates your progress along your path, however, is how you handle your mistakes.

It all comes back to balance; the god within, the god without; the good, the bad, the transforming; the knowledge, the understanding, and the action or inaction. *Wisdom comes in discerning that balance along your path, being thankful for that challenge, and remembering that road conditions can change from day to day, moment to moment.* Truthfully, that's what makes every day an adventure of body, mind, spirit, and soul.

Vulnerability

When we talk about trust, giving, and receiving, the question of vulnerability inevitably arises, usually with a negative connotation. There are moments when the strongest individual feels unsafe, when we find ourselves with no sense of comfort or defense. That vulnerability, that sense of exposure or weakness, of being used or trapped, is something to which everyone can relate.

In both our mundane and spiritual lives, avoiding vulnerability has some rather unpleasant manifestations, including:

- ‡ Being offensive and judgmental

- ‡ Avoiding group participation

- ‡ Becoming emotionally flat

- ‡ Trying too hard to please

- ‡ Putting on a social front of total command

These behaviors do not honor the sacred self. They also imply a lack of self-love and appreciation. After all, having an attitude of gratitude applies to yourself as well.

There is another side to vulnerability, however, and it's one that supports our inner God/dess. Vulnerability, applied in positive ways, allows us to explore our innermost feelings, fears, and unresolved issues. It helps us discover potential new traits for development, pursue personal and spiritual clarity, and ultimately overcome fears to take on new challenges and adventures. In short, what matters is not simply feeling vulnerable, but how we handle it.

Of the many feelings in life, vulnerability is one of those communal things. When global disaster strikes, humans everywhere relate to that moment of complete insecurity and lack of control. We respond with an outpouring of aid and compassion that is often stunning. But this kinder, gentler side would not be anywhere near as pronounced if we didn't embrace our own vulnerability, while also taking a moment to be thankful for even the smallest of blessings.

Instances of vulnerability provide us with amazing opportunities to grow closer to each other. In these moments there is no need for pretense; our humility, our generosity, our compassion, and empathy shine through without reservation. Vulnerability applied positively also:

- ‡ Improves healthy communication skills (being able to discuss needs, goals, and get assistance when needed)

- ‡ Helps resolve issues that we previously blocked

- ‡ Creates self appreciation and honest awareness (supports *know thyself*)

- ‡ Helps transform negative behavior patterns (often used as defense mechanisms)

Common sense dictates that we should not randomly trust strangers or haphazardly open up the intimate details of our life to just anyone. The ability to be vulnerable has to be adjusted according to the people or situations involved. For example, perhaps you're interested in joining a coven. You don't want to dive into just any group. The right people and harmonious energies must be present for a coven to function effectively and for it to fulfill your spiritual needs. While you'll need to open up to various groups as you visit them to see if they hold potential for you, that's different from letting down all your walls and protective instincts.

Visiting Vulnerability

Ask yourself how learning to be vulnerable in the right place and right time could help you in your spiritual growth. If you avoid being vulnerable, what are your reasons and how do you illustrate this avoidance? What personal qualities and traits do you need to develop to change that situation?

If you find that vulnerability is an aptitude on which you need to work, the next reasonable question is how? Here are some guidelines:

- ‡ Trying new things (within reason)

- ‡ Tuning into other people's feelings, and being honest about your own

- ‡ Allowing others to help you (graciously) and being ready to also help yourself as needed (like saying *no*)

- ‡ Remaining open to change

- ‡ Discovering the real reasons for negative behaviors, then avoiding those stimuli

- ‡ Speaking and listening honestly

- ‡ Releasing past fears, guilt, hostilities, and resentments

- ‡ Developing trust (when it's earned)

Last, be willing to embrace both your weaknesses and your strengths and be secure enough to honor both. This is not easy, and in many cases the quest for vulnerability comes in baby steps. My best advice is to choose what you'll work on, one thing at a time. As you work on the suggestions listed above, remain true to your ethics and philosophy. Retain your common sense. Don't give into knee-jerk reactions or societal expectations. Trust your sacred self. Walk in balance and truth.

Gracious Gratitude

Cicero (106–43 B.C.E.) wrote that, "Gratitude is not only the greatest of virtues but the parent of all others." Throughout our exploration of religious outlooks and ethics, it becomes apparent that Cicero is not the only one to ponder the importance of gratitude in a person's life. In fact, I would have to agree with his sentiments, and even go further in saying that a person and his or her spiritual path are often defined by the way in which they express gratitude. The "attitude of gratitude" is currently being examined from a psychological perspective for this very reason.

Various studies show a strong correlation between thankful living and overall well-being. People who began to write down things for which they should feel grateful became more aware of life's little gifts, which in turn led to being more thankful. Generally speaking, individuals in all walks of life who describe themselves as grateful also illustrate less stressful reactions to life, more positive outlooks, and improved vitality. They also tend to be less focused on materialism and have the capacity to find satisfaction under a wide variety of circumstances.

Beyond this, there are certain characteristics that seem to walk hand in hand in the grateful individual, such as joy and hopefulness. The thankful outlook frames a person's life experiences, including spiritual ones. Instead of filling that framework with a sense of entitlement, it acknowledges that many times other people (or situations) are responsible for the good in our lives. That includes an awareness of our inner God/dess, and the overall sense of where we fit into the big picture.

From a religious perspective, there is something about gratitude that makes a person more aware of life's web and its realities. This awareness provides more balanced expectations and proactive interactions. So why is it that modern people seem less aware of the value of gratitude in their daily life and spirituality?

At least part of the problem is the message of self-reliance. Independence is one thing, but no man is an island. We don't live alone in this world, yet we're given the feeling that we should never be indebted to anyone for anything. The sense of entitlement is contrary to positive spiritual living. We should be grateful for those who have come before, for our ancestors who forged a way in the wilderness. We should be grateful to our families and friends. Gratitude is not a means of paying a debt; it is a way of thinking and living.

Another reason people seem to be unaware of the value of gratitude is the misconception that grateful living leads to complacency. If anything, just the opposite is true. The thankful person will find the good in nearly any situation, and that awareness helps motivate change. Why remain stagnant in a tiny piece of potentially fleeting joy when specific actions could transform it into a more global fulfillment?

It may help to understand that gratitude is a mindful decision. It's not about circumstances; it's a determination to choose our life's path and appreciate all the little beauties along the way. When we're thankful for and appreciative of our life—for the sunrise, a child's laughter, the help of a stranger, even the pretty weed in the lawn, every day suddenly becomes Thanksgiving.

Thanksgiving, Pagan Style

The grateful soul is one who is ready to give and receive equally. We have often heard that it's better to give than receive, but in our spiritual reality, both have very important effects. Giving is (or should be) a natural expression of gratitude, of doing the right thing for the right reason at the right time (having a lightness of soul). Receiving is no different; it's accepting that we have needs just like everyone else (*know thyself*).

Sadly, however, there are a lot of broken souls who have problems with one or both aspects of this equation. They are afraid to give because it might engender unwanted feelings of obligation, or because the giving might not be truly appreciated (or many other possible reasons). They hesitate to receive, feeling unworthy or uncertain of showing susceptibility. We should not deny these feelings, but having an attitude of gratitude means that we also must make some very serious choices about when and where to trust, to give, and to receive (not to mention healing the parts of our soul and spirit that have been damaged).

Mindfulness and Gratitude

Think about the people in and around your life. Is there someone toward whom you've not shown gratitude who really deserves it? If so, correct that situation and watch what happens in your interactions with that person in the future.

The attitude of gratitude also creates a sense of belonging. In fact, it celebrates belonging—the kinship with all things—through kindness, charity, thoughtfulness, and compassion. This is a wonderful thing except when taken too far, as when we give a gift that isn't wanted (for whatever reason) or when it may be abused, or taking when we no longer truly have a need (or worse, taking the gift for granted). The first situation is one of which we must remain aware, but it shouldn't stop our acts of kindness. The second situation comes from individuals not walking the talk. It can be corrected once we (or they) recognize our failing. Again it's all about balance, being honest with ourselves, and looking realistically at the situation before us.

Once you begin the adventure in grateful living, it cannot help but change your life from the inside out. You'll notice that gratitude is contagious, like courtesy. Your smile, warmth, and awareness reach out and touch people.

Appreciation

A discussion of gratitude would be incomplete without discussing appreciation. When we appreciate honest efforts, good health, genuine attitudes, etc., it affirms our self-worth and the worth of others. The more we extend appreciation, the more its energy generates happiness, peace, and balance in our lives.

Internal conflict with the sacred self arises when we don't appreciate what we currently have. People often say, "I'll be happier when . . . ." This may be true, but that attitude doesn't foster abundance in the present. The goal of appreciation is one of staying in the moment and affirming whatever subtle beauties we find here.

Self-Appreciation

Learning appreciation begins with you. Each time you succeed at a spiritual goal, stop and take a moment to appreciate yourself and your progress. If you keep a spiritual diary, which I highly recommend, write down your feelings at that moment. These steps forward help build momentum for your ongoing growth.

The "as within, so without" equation also teaches us that whatever we send out we're also attracting back to ourselves. Every time we put ourselves down, speak negatively about our jobs or relationships, or lament our lack of resources, we're also unwittingly creating a magnet of negativity in our aura. Perception is ultimately the key to understanding. It's not the situation itself, but rather the way we think about our situation and handle it that creates appreciation or displeasure. Life is enhanced each time we pay attention to the good things instead of the bad.

Appreciating Your Path

Write the story of your life as it might have happened if you had never opened yourself up to your spiritual, sacred self. What would your life have been like in terms of work, relationships, family, self-images, etc.?

But appreciation is a two-way street. To show it to others, we must develop it for ourselves. See sacredness in yourself, see it in others. Appreciate yourself, appreciate others. Those simple ideals can make even the most difficult situations much more bearable. When we put our best foot forward in every thought and task, it's gratifying and maintains our spiritual integrity. It may not always be 100 percent blissful, but it's a stepping stone that can take you better places.

An appreciative outlook honors whatever happens to be on your proverbial plate. It might not be your favorite food and there may be too much or too little of it. It may not taste or look right, but it's there. Appreciate it for its potential, for the lessons it may provide. The more you do, the more you'll notice that people around you are also more appreciative. It's a positive cycle, one that you can begin at home, at work, or at play.

Charity

> Even the thought of giving, the thought of
> blessing or a simple prayer has the power to affect others.
> —Deepak Chopra

Appreciation and thankfulness go hand-in-hand with altruism. They are a natural part of the wheel of honor, respect, and gratitude. The more we experience each spoke of the wheel, the more our life is enhanced, and the more complete we find our spirits. When you appreciate what you have, when you're thankful, when you're in the moment and aware, the pressing needs of other people become obvious. The attitude of gratitude inspires our desire to spread our blessings around, which in turn generates a lot of healthful "gifting" energy.

Charity need not be extravagant to be effective. In fact, extravagance can make people feel awkward or indebted. It's little meaningful things (or things that can be done in secret) that leave a warm fuzzy feeling. It's comfort food for the soul, giving both the giver and receiver a sense of closure.

Charity is not all about money; it's about giving freely from what we have. That can mean that giving encouraging words, offering assistance without being asked, doing something without expectation of return. When you have no money to offer, how about your time? Never overlook two of the most wonderful tools in the world—your own hands. We will be talking about this more later in the book under "serving those that serve."

The beauty of giving from a heart full of gratitude is that it acts like a healing salve. When we open our hearts and have an honest desire to share, that's real power that lights up the darkness as surely as the morning sun.

Journaling

Create a gratitude journal where you can record blessings wherever you may find them. Any gifts, great or small that enrich your day should go into that book. Challenges that you overcome, people you meet, a pleasing aroma on the wind—all of these go into that book. Read your daily entry before going to bed at night and say a prayer of thanks.

Commandment 5

The Judeo-Christian Fifth Commandment teaches,
Honour thy father and thy mother: that thy days may be long
upon the land. . . .

Neo-Paganism says, Honor thy ancestors, teachers,
elders, and leaders.

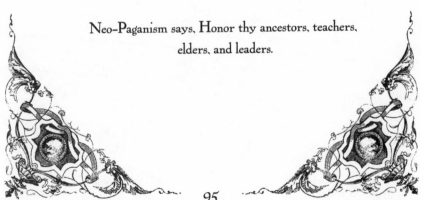

The Seeker's path is long and often meandering. There are no real roadmaps in the spiritual wilderness other than the imprint of the Divine tucked neatly into creation. Some unique individuals choose to create landmarks for us so we don't lose our way. Others trod the road and smooth it out, or run to the forefront, becoming a beacon and inspiration, so we don't trip and fall. Others still, hearing the many voices just finding their way to the Path, come back down the road. These wise ones smile gently and reach out a hand, offering companionship and guidance as to what's ahead. The Seeker sighs gratefully and welcomes the company.

The road can be lonely, but we are truly never alone. The God/dess within and without holds us close. The ancestors hover between the worlds to watch and guide. The elders make our path easier, and teachers and leaders open the way for other Seekers to find their stride. Let us walk together in peace.

Honor Thy Ancestors, Teachers, Elders, and Leaders

Respect is earned. Those who are living a prayerful and grateful life are those whom we will begin to respect. There are a lot of people who have walked this path before us, some of whom gave their lives so we could enjoy the freedoms we enjoy and others who have made the path smoother by their works, insights, and actions. Nonetheless, we live in a world where old often equals outmoded. We have lost touch with the wisdom of the ancestors. We often forget that those who serve today need to be respected. The goal of this chapter is to ponder our responsibility to our leaders, elders, and ancestors.

Ancestors

It has been said that those who do not learn from history are doomed to repeat it. History moves in cycles; war and peace, growth and stagnation, prosperity and poverty, and everything "old" eventually surfaces in new ways. We have the cycles of history to thank (in part) for the emergence of Neo-Paganism, as well as for many thinkers, philosophers, and pathfinders who made their way through a world that has not always been kind to them. These people, and others whose names we may never know, have left their footprints. Their legacy still sings to us.

Honoring the ancestors takes two basic forms. The first is showing devotion, gratitude, and respect to our own familial ancestors, and the second is by honoring all ancestors (or the general ancestral spirit), such as community elders who have passed over and the founders of our traditions. While Neo-Pagans and Wiccans do not actually worship the ancestors in the manner that's found in Santaria or Voudon, ancestor worship is worth examining because of its long history.

Ancestor Worship

Worship of personal or communal ancestors is a form of religious expression that has appeared in a wide variety of nations, including China, Africa, Malaysia, Polynesia, Egypt, Greece, and Rome. Even the Hebrews showed reverence for the dead. The most common reason for ancestor worship is that the deceased continue to have interest in the affairs of the living. When we honor them, we placate their angry spirits. Further, many believe that the ancestors are willing to be helpful to the living by giving advice or sharing wisdom, just as guardian angels and spirit guides do. At this juncture, it's important to separate "ghosts" from "ancestral spirits." While there are various rituals for communicating with ghosts, they are not generally regarded with the same respect as the ancestors (who have fully crossed over, whereas the ghost may be stuck between lives).

> Every man is a quotation from all his ancestors.
> —Ralph Waldo Emerson

While the ancestors have crossed over, most societies that practiced ancestor worship (or reverence) felt that these beings still remained close, especially to their kin. People believed that praying to, or appeasing, the ancestors could create manifestations that included rain, fertility, joy, etc. Other means through which the ancestors are known to communicate include dreams, divination tools, vision quests, and even possession.

The most positive social aspect of ancestor worship was the sense of family solidarity. When it comes to honoring personal ancestors, this focus still holds great merit, but how do we begin? First, it's important to recognize that honoring these beings is not the same as worshipping them. Unless your path stresses worship, it need not enter into your personal practices.

Definitions according to Webster's

Honor: the esteem due or paid to worth. High estimation, reverence, veneration. A testimony of esteem. Dignity, reputation, or a sense of what is just, right and true.

Worship: short for WORTH-ship. The state (or quality) of being worthy and honorable. Paying supreme respect (often to the Divine) or performing acts of adoration and veneration.

We can see from these definitions that honoring our ancestors can be remembrance or commemoration. It can also be something far more religious in nature, even a type of communion. In a Neo-Pagan setting, the remembrance-commemoration approach is more common; such as setting up a family ancestral altar during Hallows (Samhain/Halloween) as a way of remembering those who came before and their importance to us today. There are many other ways to honor personal ancestral spirits, including:

✝ Sharing the teachings or crafts passed down to you by them with friends and family so these valuable things are not lost to time.

✝ Holding small rituals of blessing and peace on special dates and enjoying your memories. Note that before or after the ritual, you may wish to have a meal of some of the ancestor's favorite foods. You can also burn incense of a scent you know he or she liked.

✝ Looking at photographs and other images of these people regularly, allowing all the special moments with them to bless you once again. Don't forget to share those moments through stories with others who will treasure them.

✝ Maintaining a memory book filled with stories about your ancestors, their sayings, and habits, and other memorabilia. (This book will become a family heirloom.)

✝ Creating an ancestral altar filled with pictures, memorabilia, and candles.

I realize some readers may be wondering what honoring our personal ancestors has to do with ethics. They connect on many levels. Each time we see or think about our ancestors, we're also bringing to mind the valuable lessons and traditions they gave us. This preserves their teachings for the future. Since ours is a living tradition, this preservation becomes a bridge, and the foundations, lessons, and advancements of the past build toward a secure and well-grounded future.

What about our ancestors in a broader sense, the ancients, the founders of our nation or tradition? What is our responsibility to them? There's a certain cohesiveness between personal ancestors and global ancestors. We are still showing respect for what these people have given us; we are still passing along and continuing their tradition (culturally, familially, and spiritually). While Neo-Pagans as a whole are a very innovative lot, the power of tradition should not be ignored. Consider the communal power any one custom holds as a result of its being reenacted by hundreds (if not thousands) of people over decades. Take even something simple like knocking on wood for luck. While this probably has roots in ancient tree worship (Druidic ties), many people continue to follow the custom believing it holds lucky energy. That's a lot of raw energy just waiting to be tapped.

> Each Ancestor, while traveling through the country,
> was thought to have scattered a trail of words and musical
> notes along the line of his footprints . . . . A song was both
> map and direction finder. Providing you knew the song, you
> could always find your way across country. . . .
> —Bruce Chatwin

Tradition reflects on who we have been as a people. Be it spiritual or mundane, history creates a sense of what inspires and motivates us, a sense of what is truly important. Even in a brave new world, there are values and goals that are timeless.

Sample Ancestor Prayer
(This is an adaptation of a Kwanza prayer to the ancestors.) Our great ancestors who are among us, we humbly offer thanks for the many blessings you have given. We extend our love toward you, and our gratitude, for all you endured so we could have a better life. Mothers of our many nations, Fathers of all people, we invoke you to lead and guide us to higher understandings. Help us discover our full potential and our love for all peoples. Ancestors, guide us toward unity, guide us with strong values, help us show respect and kindness; help us learn and make our families stronger. We swear upon all we hold dear to uphold and sustain this earth, and to continue to strive for spiritual liberation.

Ancestors—from all corners of creation, I/we welcome you among us. Thank you for all that you have done to pave the way for a better future for all humankind. By all your honored names we each remember you in our hearts today, and welcome your continued guidance in daily life. Bless us, walk with us, watch over those we love and help us ever continue to strive for spiritual insight. Today and every day you are with us, in our hearts and memories.

There is still some debate as to whether the global ancestors should be worshipped. Many argue they were mortal beings who are more than likely still on the reincarnation wheel. This means that they're not higher beings, and the general opinion is if they were not higher beings, they are not worthy of worship in a religious sense. That doesn't mean we shouldn't respect them and celebrate what they have left for us. But in the face of the commandment, "thou art God/dess," worshipping another human spirit may have serious limits and faults. If that spirit has an agenda, if he or she has all-too-human failings, there's little worship can produce other than perhaps a greater communion and understanding of that person. It is also uncertain as to whether an ascended or divine being would have any need for worship.

The most common way the Neo-Pagan community honors ancestors in ritual, particularly during times of the year (such as Samhain) is when the veil between the worlds grows thin. Other times may be holidays like Presidents' Day, which is a perfect opportunity to remember our former leaders and to pray for leaders everywhere. Both of these are options that you can consider integrating into your own practice, as inspiration dictates.

Ancestor Altar

Begin assembling items for an ancestor altar. Decide if it's going to honor your family ancestors, global ancestors, or both. Find a good place to set up the altar. In some spiritual traditions, the dead reside in a mysterious region in the west, so perhaps you can set up your ancestor altar against a west wall. Also consider what spells, rituals, and other commemorations you're going to start weaving into your life with this special space in mind.

Whatever you do to honor ancestors, please remember the people who made you, you and the people who made us, us. They deserve to be cherished in our thoughts, and honored in our actions. By so doing, we can create a future that applies valuable lessons that we may eventually evolve from temporal humankind to eternal spiritkind by completely activating the inner god-self and divine potentials.

Teachers

What of those individuals that have become our spiritual teachers? What does honoring them mean and how do we know which teachers are truly "good" and "ethical" and therefore worthy of respect? These are hard questions to answer. Let's start by defining the basics of what qualifies as a good teacher in mundane terms.

Good Teachers

Good teachers tend to:

‡ Feel attracted to teaching early in life (often by their teens). Some become student aids and peer helpers in school.

‡ Set high, but obtainable, goals for students.

‡ Don't simply "talk at" students, but create an interactive environment.

‡ Learn about each student's strengths, goals, and weaknesses, and how each person learns best (verbally, mechanically, visually, etc.).

✝ Have strong skills and knowledge about the subject matter he or she presents.

✝ Plan their instructions so as to include obtainable benchmarks for success.

✝ Provide ongoing evaluation, assessment, and input.

✝ Motivate learning through proactive methods (like peer-to-peer projects).

✝ Create safe environments for students that honor diversity.

✝ Have well-managed sessions that are consistent and fair to participants.

✝ Promote applied learning in the community.

✝ Commit to lifelong learning (personal and professional).

This list is a very good measure of a spiritual teacher, too. We might add that spiritual teachers should be guides, not manipulators. A teacher provides basic framework and functional ideas, but each student must bring their own crayons with which to color their spirituality. The ethical spiritual teacher helps others reach the "Aha!" moment without necessarily spoon-feeding the student. The very young spiritual seeker might need milk toast for a while, but eventually they hunger for meat, and meat always tastes better if you've successfully earned it. More importantly, when that "Aha!" moment comes, the teacher compliments the student on the accomplishment, rather than trying to take credit for it!

Spiritual teachers must walk carefully. Teachers have to watch emotional responses in their students. It's not uncommon to have a kind of idol or guru worship develop, and any kind of teacher worship needs to be nipped in the bud as early as possible. We are all God/dess. A good teacher becomes a helpmate to a person's reconnection with, and expression of, divine energy. A good teacher provides foundational and challenging materials so the groundwork is strong, and the student always has something for which to strive.

It's no wonder, then, that when you find such teachers they're usually in pretty high demand. Bear in mind, however, that the best teachers are not always those whose names you've heard a hundred times. Fame doesn't necessarily imply good teaching skills; it more likely implies good PR. In fact, the wallflowers of our community sometimes become amazing educators if they receive positive reinforcement and a good foundation for themselves.

For example, say you come across someone in your community who has been around for several years, but has for the most part worked behind the scenes. After a conversation or two, you discover this person has a wonderful way of touching your heart. As the saying goes, the teacher will appear when the student is ready. If you're looking for a teacher, look for one with the characteristics we've discussed, but don't give into the fame game. Finding a good teacher is worth your time.

How do you honor the special teachers in your life? Mostly by thanking them and living in such a way that it gives them joy to observe you. Teachers are like parents who strive to give their child a sense of independence. At long last the kids walk, talk, and think for themselves. Beyond that, tell others who need a teacher of this person, remember him or her on special days with a card or phone call, and share the lessons he or she gave you with others, giving credit where credit is due.

The "Bad" Teacher

It would be remiss to talk about teachers in our community without touching on those whose ethics and methods are questionable. I don't think it's a secret that overblown egos exist in many spiritual and religious settings. In Wicca, this occurs partly because we're such a highly individualized group. Teaching too much from ego (constantly feeling above or better than your students) may to lead to dogma, deter individuality, and stifle free thought in students.

Teachers who operate from dubious principles bring shame to more than just themselves; they reflect badly on the entire community and any deity they presume to serve. The predatory and power-hungry aspects of such individuals come as a sharp counterbalance to true teachers who share light and healing. The question our community must face, therefore, is how can we ethically weed out bad teachers when a favorite Neo-Pagan phrase tells us that "it's all good."

To weed out the bad teachers, perhaps we must first realize it's *not* "all good" when you're talking about the "good of all." We have a responsibility to warn about, and turn the uncomfortable spotlight on, teachers whose personal agendas, negative characteristics, etc., shadows their teaching. Just as you wouldn't want someone walking blindly into a poison ivy patch, you don't want them walking blindly into the hands of an unethical teacher. Tell your stories truthfully and admit your biases. The truth should speak for itself and not need the embellishment of anger or outrage. However, if after a balanced warning a person still makes the choice to study with a bad teacher, we can only honor the student's free will by saying, "So be it."

A bad teacher's main value seems to be in showing us how not to behave. The harsh and often painful lessons that happen to students of these teachers certainly seem long-lasting, but at what cost? Each of us is given the ability to avoid being a victim. After all, thou art God/dess! Each of us can express our sacredness in far more positive ways (as within, so without), and each of us can take a stand against wrongs (the power of place). At the same time, we cannot force anyone else to do what we're doing.

By taking control over our own life and walking with integrity, each of us leads and teaches by example. That means being clear and establishing our standards and expectations as a community. For example, I think we can all agree that it is not acceptable to use coven members like they were slave labor (and demean them when they balk at being ordered around). Bossing is one facet of bad teaching by someone who has unrealistic expectations and an inflated ego. We don't hear about this happening as much as we used to, perhaps because we (the community) as a whole spoke out and said, "Enough!"

The same communal behaviors/reactions hold true in what we expect of our teachers and leaders, now and in the future. We must be consistent in our standards and reflect them in how we live. As we do, people around us become aware of ethical living through our example. At that point, it becomes difficult for the bad teacher to remain hidden, let alone continue their abuse.

It does us no good as a community to remain silent about bad teachers and what they do. We cannot simply sweep problematic individuals under the rug; eventually some poor soul trips on the rug. I believe that when we are as certain as humanly possible about a wrong, and do nothing to resolve it, we become likewise culpable. What exactly can you do? I advise an elemental approach:

Air: Talk to this teacher (think *tough love*). Not everyone realizes the traps they've fallen into until someone tosses them a lifeline. They can accept or reject your insights, but you've at least put forth the effort.

Fire: Pray and work nonmanipulative magick for the individual. Send energy that they can accept or reject. Ask the divine to guide them to better ways of living and being.

Water: Be open about your opinions about the individual, but carefully weigh them against what you know for a fact and have personally experienced (documentation helps). If we want to clean up dirt and get support for our efforts, our own backyards have to be pretty well above reproach. Note the difference between speaking an honest opinion and spreading rumors. Don't give into the temptation to do the latter, for it may undermine the strength of your observations with perceived pettiness.

Earth: Remain professional. This isn't a time for catfights, name-calling, and stomping like a spoiled seven-year-old. If you want your observations to be taken seriously, you have to act like a real adult. Ground and focus, then speak or act.

At the end of the day, it stands to reason that you may or may not be successful, but at least you will have tried. That effort helps keep your life's Wheel in balance and maintains harmony with the sacred self. It also engenders positive vibrations in and around your life, vibrations of honor, respect, truthfulness, tact, and wisdom.

Leaders

When talking about teachers, it helps to expand our discussion to include our leaders and spiritual facilitators, the movers and shakers of our community. In any important movement in history, there have been people who stepped up to the tasks of leadership. Some leaders did so out of a sense of justice, others out of drive, others out of the need to be needed. Some succeeded, some failed. Neo-Paganism is no different, and our community is certainly not immune to the leaders who step up for the wrong reasons.

Before pondering the negatives, let's first examine what makes for a good leader and role model. Most effective leaders have:

- ‡ Trusted allies and positive role models to whom they can turn for help in decision-making

- ‡ Strong principles that drive action (*who* is right is not so important as *what* is right)

- ‡ A willingness to admit errors and then work to correct that error (i.e., FIX IT)

- ‡ Constructive criticism to offer alongside supportive encouragement

- ‡ A fully awakened sense of responsibility and culpability

- ‡ The capacity to know when they need help, and ask for it

- ‡ Good communication skills

- ‡ A plan (but they don't "marry" themselves to it so much that there's no flexibility)

✝ Insights into what motivates people (be that ethics, emotions, logic, pride, self-image or whatever)

✝ A talent for making complex things simple (describe tasks in a form others can understand and execute)

✝ The ability to listen and observe, then use the information gathered

✝ Ways of acting that harmonize with the goals or ideals being presented (they lead by example)

✝ Commitment, even in the face of delays and setbacks

✝ Strength to tell the hard truths (tough love)

✝ An aptitude for helping people adjust to difficult changes

✝ Confidence, humility, and pragmatism (*know thyself*)

✝ A disposition that inspires improved performance

✝ A willingness to complete tasks, and/or to delegate, knowing that two hands are not always enough

✝ Timeliness (being late is incredibly unprofessional, not to mention rude—no Pagan Standard Time, please)

✝ Visibility and accessibility

Leadership is about unlocking people's potential and then guiding that potential for the benefit of an individual, a group, an organization, or even the entire world. By knowing themselves (their values, priorities, etc.), effective leaders can identify ethical potentialities, make ethical choices, and commit to seeing through that choice.

Reading the list of qualifications given above can easily intimidate some people. Leadership is a "big thing," and not everyone was meant to lead. Nevertheless, an honest person who strives to be his or her best inspires the best in others. Someone who is confident in their spirituality and willing to live that spirituality certainly has the potential to lead. Thou art God/dess.

A "bad" leader, on the other hand, is one who thinks he or she knows everything and can micromanage people into submission. He or she promotes the self over the goal or the group and avoids taking responsibility but often steals praise. Also, bad leaders will typically resist change, are slow to hear advice (let alone act on it), and eventually create enmity between himself or herself and anyone perceived as a "threat."

> It doesn't take a majority to make a rebellion;
> it takes only a few determined leaders and a sound cause.
> —H. L. Mencken

Those who can, should. Those who cannot, should support a good leader. Support through words and actions are ideal ways to honor such an individual. But we should also remember that our leaders, no matter how good, are also human beings with real needs and failings. Recognizing their humanity is also a way of honoring them. It has often been said, "To whom much is given, much is expected." However, I would also say, "From whom much comes, much should also be returned." Which brings up the next important point: service.

What Makes a Good Teacher or Leader

Make a list of the people in your life you consider to have been good teachers. What qualities made them different from other teachers? After reviewing this list meditate on the qualities of a teacher or leader you feel you possess. Do you feel you'd ever want to teach or lead? Why or why not?

Serving Those Who Serve

Those of us who do not fill the roles of teacher, clergy, elder, or leader have responsibilities to those who do. We owe them honor, respect, and gratitude. It is no accident that many of our community's greatest voices and hands have suffered burnout at least once, if not several times. This happens because all too often the community takes without giving back. While this is predictable in a community that is growing very rapidly and where there are lots of spiritually hungry people waiting to be fed, it's a situation that must be remedied. If we truly treasure and honor our leaders, we will want them to be working from a space of fullness, and we will want them around for a very long time.

I know that our leaders and teachers seem to be complete, in control, and competent. That's because they're good at what they do! But their competence can give the impression that there's nothing we can possibly offer them. Realistically, however, we're looking at authentic human beings who have ongoing needs, just like we do. So the next question becomes, how can we return service? How can we refill our leaders with all the energies they expend for our community?

First consider the roots of the word "serve." In Latin, it has several meanings, including burdens or weight, and to keep from harm. Definitions of the English word include "to wait, deliver or attend, to help by good office, to provide for wants and needs, to regulate personal behavior, and to provide contentment." This gives us plenty of ideas from which to begin pondering personal actions.

Service need not be grand to be meaningful. Anything that lifts a leader's burdens a little, or offsets a potentially negative situation, is a great gift. I remember one speaker who was traveling with her children. The children were being normal children, her hands were full. Her son needed his shoe tied. Before she could even blink, I swooped down and took care of the task. Was that grand and awe inspiring? Heck, no. But I can tell you that she still talks about that moment, which tells me it was a "good" service.

Want some other ideas? Begin by being observant. Does the leader, teacher, or speaker enjoy coffee in the morning? Perhaps you can have a cup ready and waiting at his or her first class. This simple gesture is so thoughtful that it brings a smile and provides that person with a sense of being truly appreciated.

Does the leader have children on board at an event? Offer to help with them or watch them for a while so her hands and mind are freed up for the tasks at hand. These are examples of physical service. Others include carrying books for an author, relieving a weary registration person for an hour, taking a pick-up-trash walk, offering to clean the bathrooms at a site so someone else doesn't have to, carrying firewood, helping set up tents, and so forth. While at first these seem like insignificant tasks, what happens when you have five, ten, or fifty people offering this kind of service to our leaders and facilitators?

Emotional service comes in the form of hugs, and the honest statement of appreciation. Tell a teacher, "Thank you for a great festival, it helped me a lot," or, "Thank you for that class, I understand things much more clearly now." Gratitude has an amazing capacity to heal and revitalize even the weariest speaker or teacher. Emotional service may also take the form of listening. Many leaders, because they travel, don't know people intimately in the community they're visiting. That leaves them without confidantes and sounding boards. If you find yourself in a position of being able to listen, with or without feedback, give it a try. You may just make a life-long friend.

Mental service is similar to physical service. I see this as efforts like offering to take over the updates for a Web site, doing research for a project or event, assisting in a class, doing anything else that actively engages the mind. Mental activity takes time and energy, so what you're effectively doing is freeing up a little of both for the leader to whom you offer these services.

> Leadership has a harder job to do than
> just choose sides. It must bring sides together.
> —Rev. Jesse Jackson

What about spiritual service? Remember your leaders and facilitators in your rituals, prayers, spells, and meditations. Send energy their way often. Whisper their names on the winds, sing them to the stars (names have power). And when practicable, invite them to join you in these celebrations so that their hearts and spirits can be refilled.

Finally, we come to financial service. This is where things get very dicey among Neo-Pagans. There is a huge divide in our community between those who feel it's inherently wrong to accept money for spiritual teaching and service, and those who think payment is simply another form of energy exchange. I personally am in the latter group. In times past, you might have brought bread, a blanket, or some other form of useful exchange to someone (like a midwife) who was teaching you a skill or providing you a service. Currency—real money—is just an updated form of this tradition. It's not as colorful or imaginative, but it is functional nonetheless.

Consider for a moment that teachers and leaders have to take time out of their normal day (which might include a paying job, arranging for child care, etc.) to be working in the community. Now if that time is only a little here and a little there, I can see doing it as a love offering. However, most of these people invest enough time in the community for that effort to be equal to a part-time or full-time job. So either we find ways for these valued individuals to feed their families and pay their bills while helping us, or we give up the right to ask them for so much time and effort.

We cannot have it both ways. It's incredibly thoughtless to presume that any person should be able to give time and energy to the community, hold down a day job, and still find time for their own family, let alone their personal spirituality. It's simply not reasonable. And it's no less reasonable for those among us that we consider our priests/priestesses to be our ministers and clergy.

Pagan Clergy

The positive characteristics for Pagan or Wiccan clergy are very similar to those for our teachers and leaders. However, working clergy need to fulfill other qualifications, not the least of which is some level of training in psychology (such as effective counseling methods) and theology (particularly apologetics—

the defense of a position using symantics). Presently, most of our priests and priestesses do not have those kinds of training, which are ethically vital to their role within and without our groups.

That's partly the case because we are spiritual practitioners without churches. There have been few accredited Neo-Pagan higher education centers or Neo-Pagan seminaries. I pray that this situation will change, but without establishing a continuity; a cornerstone of our faith that shares a basic vision and focus, I suspect such things will continue to be slow in coming.

Other traits that set apart effective clergy include compassion, empathy, good people skills, diplomacy, and the ability to keep a confidence. Beyond this foundation, our outstanding priests, priestesses, ministers, and clergy have a true higher calling that drives them forward. Such callings are sometimes situational, others are for a lifetime.

Say, for example, a friend comes to you with devastating news: they have a terminal illness. They ask you to act as a priest or priestess for their rite of passage. You may not be trained for this . . . but such a heartfelt request isn't one easily dismissed. This is an example of a situational calling.

Other people, however, know beyond any doubt that their purpose is to serve our community in a truly religious and spiritual sense. They are "married" to the community. They teach, they guide, they hold us when we cry, and dance with us in our joys. It takes a rare breed of person to accept this position and truly *live it*. That brings us back to the topic of money. How can we possibly have full-time ministers if they have no means of support? Consider: it takes money just to rent a space for ongoing meetings and rituals, let alone buy ritual supplies. While donations might cover that part of the equation, are we really comfortable in the thought that some of our clergy are going home to huge debts, pending evictions, and no medical insurance?

Paid Pagan Clergy?

Ponder: Do you feel that having paid pagan clergy is a good idea? If so, how do you feel that goal could be manifest?

If we want our clergy at our beck and call, we have to find a way to regularly provide for them. Ministers of other faiths all over the world receive financial support, free or reduced-cost housing, food offerings, etc. In the United States, they also get tax breaks. Unfortunately, because the Neo-Pagan community does not have one or several large infrastructures into which money is always flowing, this makes it hard to find a way to make full-time paid clergy a reality. That doesn't mean we should stop talking about it.

There are still ways we can help our clergy. If you know a teacher or priest/ess whom you respect and who is in need:

‡ Send them a money order anonymously or drop a bag of groceries or bundle of firewood at their home.

‡ If that person has a business, service, or art, support it. Go shopping early for Yule.

‡ Pick up clothing and school supplies for that leader's kids, even secondhand.

‡ Network the known need around the community to others who have been blessed by this person.

Find a way to turn things around. If there is one thing Neo-Pagans know how to do well, it's networking.

Elders

I left our elders to the end of this chapter for many reasons. First, they may (or may not) be teachers, leaders, facilitators, or clergy, which puts them into an interesting niche. No matter what function an elder has filled during their time in our community, they are still our elders. Now, I am the first to admit that there are some elders (such as Aleister Crowley) toward whom I have trouble mustering respect and gratitude, but I also have to remind myself that these people were walking the path in far different times—times when they used shock value as a means of getting some type of recognition.

Compared to other religions, ours is young. Nonetheless, we are now entering a second and perhaps third generation of Neo-Pagans who have been brought up in some type of magickal tradition, and some witches claim longer lineages.

Stop, Look, Respond

Look around: are there elders in need in your community? If so, how can you help them? Don't debate or wait—get busy. It's fairly safe to say that there is not one Neo-Pagan community that doesn't have at least one older member who is struggling to pay the rent or buy groceries. As far as I know, we have no Wiccan or Pagan retirement homes, no religious retirement funds, no food shuttles, and very few organized pagan elder-care outreach programs. Some of this work is done by individuals who see the need and care, but that simply is not enough.

Eventually, if we live long enough, we will be the elders of the community. While we may hope that our life has led to a secure retirement fund and a family that will help us in our old age, the reality is that we have a lot of alternative lifestyles in our community, and some of us do not have legal family structures. We also have elders who have not had the luxury of ongoing day jobs that provide pensions or other benefits. In fact, some of these people devoted their time to our community instead of taking cushy jobs that gave them medical insurance.

I believe we need to begin to care for our elders by creating established Neo-Pagan charities and outreach programs that have sound planning and strong infrastructures. Rather than treating yourself to that pretty crystal or souped-up athame, put the money into funds that support pagans. Or give it to an elder in need privately or anonymously (and encourage other people to do likewise). If you're strapped financially, give your local elders some of your free time. Invite them out to lunch or drive them to a doctor's appointment if they can no longer do so. Help clean the house or just provide some good company. Remember that these people not only represent our community's past, but they are the foundation upon which our future is being built. The saying goes, "a chain is only as strong as its weakest link." By supporting our elders, we are making the chain of pagans stronger and casting it into a more secure future for all of us.

6 Commandment

The Judeo-Christian Sixth Commandment instructs,
Thou shalt not kill.

Neo-Paganism says, All life is sacred.

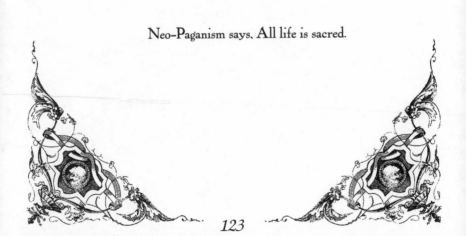

Anew wind whispers across the land as a baby cries, and welcomes its first breath. Elsewhere a flower blossoms, a whale breaches the surface, a dog bays at the moon, a lazy cat stretches in a sun puddle, the last ember of a campfire flickers, and a leaf floats out to sea. Yet in another corner of the world, a mother and father tuck sleepy children into bed, a village's last lights go dark, crickets serenade the stars, and even trees seem to yawn. The Wheel has turned. This is Gaia. This is life.

The wind moves on, blowing a sailboat of wishes across a sea. It moves further still—beyond the docks, beyond the sand, all the way to the next horizon and greets the morning. There, between the dark and light, the sounds and silences, the Seeker also waits. This new wind wraps around the Seeker in invisible strength. Soon, the air is part of that person, with the fires of dawn, the salt of the sea, and the earth beneath the seeker's feet. They are part of it; they are one with it. The Wheel moves on. This is life. This is sacred.

All Life Is Sacred

$\mathfrak{I}$t is truly sacred ground upon which we walk every day. Respect for nature and every inhabitant of this planet is part of living our path. With that in mind, the prudent witch not only "does unto others" . . . but also does unto the earth as he or she would wish to be treated. Reclaiming this sense of sacredness in the concrete jungle, however, isn't an easy task. Nor is measuring how our actions affect the entire planet—which might affect the many situations and decisions we face. Let's examine life's sacredness together to find some perspective.

Animal, Vegetable, and Mineral Sacredness

We talked a little about the sanctity of nature earlier. Our world is, indeed, a gift. For a while, it seemed that humankind tried to work cooperatively with nature, but a yearning to make life easier and a sense of entitlement crept in. Somewhere along the line, we ceased being faithful stewards of our world and became dominionists. Whatever we could harvest, hunt, cut down, float over, reach, and pick—all of it became "fair game."

"Fair game." Who determines fair? Who made the rules? When exactly did living in reciprocity with nature become a game instead of the serious business of survival? Probably right around the time that life spans became longer thanks to scientific advancements. When humankind no longer needed to worry so much about survival, our slow separation from nature and callous attitude toward it developed. This is an excellent example of what happens when what was once sacred becomes a matter of apathy, or worse, gets taken totally for granted.

Let's take the example of plant spirits. At one time, the making of wine and beer (from grain and hops) was a sacred occupation, often left to clergy. Anyone who "abused" the plant spirits suffered for it (e.g., a hangover or addiction). In fact, it was considered very unseemly by many ancient standards to exploit libations. Many fermented brews were intended for the sacred altar and treated with all due reverence.

Now, however, things are much different. Alcoholic beverages are big business, and the idea of wine as a sacred beverage has dramatically decreased. Correlation? Well, a large number of the individuals killed in automobile accidents are killed in accidents caused by drunk driving. This indicates that the respect for these beverages has been lost. This is not to say that alcohol cannot be enjoyed without disrespecting tradition. The key here is responsible use, and honoring the energies of everything we consume. This is one of the reasons I advocate reintroducing prayer to the family dining table. It gives us a moment to be mindful of our foods, beverages, and blessings.

Plant and Mineral Power
Meditate on the concept of plant and mineral spirits then answer these questions:

‡ Do plants have "feelings"? If so, does it hurt the grass when we walk on it or mow it? If not, do you feel there is an overall spirit in nature (why or why not)?

‡ What lessons or symbols from the plant and mineral world affect you most deeply? Why?

‡ If you were a plant or a mineral, what would you be?

‡ Is it acceptable to mine the earth for stones that we're just enjoying as a trinket rather than using (such as a quartz in a watch)?

Mineral Morals

What about the mineral world? We've certainly seen what human greed in the quest for more oil sources has done locally and globally. While one person or group avoids all efforts at finding alternative energy sources, we venture seemingly without any apology into the untouched regions ready, willing, and able to destroy habitats and further tear at life's web for oil. It's a pity, and it could be changed with research into alternative energies, but that's not profitable. Again, we've lost the balance, and we've lost sight of how our behavior will affect future generations.

On a smaller scale, what about all those pretty shiny things we Neo-Pagans adore? Is it wholly ethical to have made them into "big business?" I love my jewelry and rocks as much as the next person, but when I see the price tag on some, my first reaction is, *it's just a rock!* There is likely very little harm to finding and keeping items that the earth gives up willingly, like a smoky quartz crystal in a stream. But what about mining for those items, especially ones that aren't really used in daily life other than as an aesthetic pleasure? What is the right best thing for the minerals? Balance, forward thinking, and reciprocity are concepts that must be applied to the mining of our resources as well as to the earth overall.

Animal Realms

The desire for balance and reciprocity may also account for the number of vegetarians in our community. They choose to respect the sacredness of animal life and abstain from that food group. While not all Neo-Pagans are vegetarians, most can understand that perspective and also share their own views from a similar point of respectfulness.

Life in nature feeds on life. That's a reality. Humans have canine teeth, indicating that our physiology is designed for meat-eating. Now, thanks to the wonder of our reasoning minds and availability of alternative foods, we can think past that natural drive and choose something different. However, if we make a decision to go vegetarian, we must also supplement our bodies with the nutrients we need that would otherwise be fulfilled by meat. That is one way we can respect the animal kingdom, and honor the temple of our own body.

So why do so many Neo-Pagans or Wiccans remain meat-eaters? Many see it as natural. Instead of giving up meat altogether, many of us have regular meatless meals, and thank the spirits of the animals that give us our meat when we consume it.

A second path of thought with regard to animal sacredness is that of how human interactions with nature help or harm creatures. If you've ever seen pictures of birds and sea animals covered in crude oil, you know how disturbing those images are. That is but one example of how humans have changed natural dynamics, and how our presence affects animals. It's also an excellent illustration of how the kingdoms of this earth interact; in this case animal, mineral, and human. Another example of this is hunting for sport.

The discussion of animal sacredness also leads down a third avenue to the ethics of keeping pets, training animals, and performing experiments on animals. Biologically speaking, we know that humans are members of the animal kingdom. At least in the modern world, most people would never consider keeping people as "pets" or experimenting on them without their consent. So where does this leave us with animals who seem to have a certain level of intelligence and problem-solving ability? Consider:

- Dogs can instinctively find their way across the country, and use canine skills to save someone they love without being directed.

- Apes have learned sign language and show remarkable parental abilities.

- The octopus appears to have the ability to express feelings and show curiosity.

- Dolphins answer yes or no questions using specifically located panels. They also learned to place a ball in a floating basket. However, when the dolphin was given the ball without a basket and told to put it where it belonged, the dolphin moved to the "no" panel. This was not a taught response, and it was not created through any type of genetic manipulation.

Do we as a species have the right to use these creatures and others like them however we wish? It's not my intention to over-anthropomorphize, but it's prudent to recognize that we cannot say with absolute certainty that nature has not developed any creature other than humans with the ability to reason or develop reasoning skills. The more we study the world's wonders, the more we discover that there is much we do not yet know, including creatures we never knew existed. That alone elicits a sense of caution. Additionally, if we assume that we're projecting human behavior onto various creatures, is it possible that we're over-looking some types of naturally intelligent behavior in animals (including the potential for growth and learning)? For example, we may assume that dogs are loyal because that's what we have come to expect from domesticated canines. But in nature dogs run in packs and may defend that group when confronted. Is this a kind of loyalty or is it simply defending territory? How we interpret animals depends on our perspectives of behavior.

We probably won't discover the complete answer to such questions for a while, especially as we extend our research out-ward from this world to other words (which I ponder later in this chapter under Celestial Sacredness). In the meanwhile, from a philosophical standpoint, the question of choice comes to bear in our ethical behaviors toward the animal kingdom. For exam-ple, many Neo-Pagans have pets that may not have chosen to be taken into their owners' homes. Not all of those homes are set up in such a way as to be healthy and positive for the animal (like a large energetic dog being put in a small apartment. As we go about taking in creatures, our ethical choice is clear: we must take care of these creatures in a loving, responsible way.

Scientists are performing experiments with animals in the effort to improve the human animal's life. The question remains: How much injury are we willing to inflict on creatures to whom we give no choice? And what's the karmic reprisal? What happens when we breach the divide between species. We are already experiencing what happens when we've so extended the human lifespan that population rages out of control.

Since most of us are not research scientists, exactly where our responsibility lies for finding reasonable and informed answers to the foregoing questions is uncertain. We do, however, need to think about these situations, especially when regulatory questions about animal research come to a popular or regional vote. Ultimately, we have to design a personal response that we can live with for a long time, and one that honors our inner God/dess.

Animals in Review

After pondering animal sacredness, ask yourself these questions:

‡ Do you feel you'll treat your pets (if you have them) differently than before? If so, in what ways?

‡ When, if ever, do you feel animal experimentation is acceptable?

‡ Are you a meat-eater? Why or why not?

Personal Sacredness

Speaking of "thou art God/dess," once we accept that all life is sacred, it's natural to take the next step and accept ourselves as sacred beings. The average person, however, doesn't really think of himself in those terms. We can see ourselves in other descriptive terms like "mothering," "playful," "hard-working," etc., but sacred? When we first get up in the morning experiencing dry mouth and bed head, the last thing we're likely to feel is religious or holy.

Perhaps at least part of the problem is a lack of deep-knowingness about what constitutes sacredness. "Sacred" doesn't mean "perfect," for example. When most people envision a sacred being, however, they think of bright, glowing, impeccableness. That's a tough act to follow. So in thinking about personal sacredness, let's first ponder the meaning of this word in the broadest sense from Webster's.

‡ To be dedicated

‡ To be set apart (as not profane or common), remain inviolable often through a religious ritual such as consecration

‡ To be sane and safe

Once you dedicate yourself to a specific religious path and ethical structure, you've engaged the sacred self. This is not something reserved for an elite few. It's part of human nature but remains dormant until we start our spiritual reawakening process.

Second, by living as spiritually awakened beings we set ourselves apart from the sheeple (the sheep-people, a term I invented in Chapter 1 to describe the mindless followers who want their life and choices dictated to them). In that moment, we become our own guru and priest/ess. We start recognizing our special uniqueness and celebrating it. In turn, we also honor each person's right to likewise celebrate the self and personal vision. In short, our goal becomes that of being better human beings, individually and collectively. In Wicca, this choice is often marked by a ritual of dedication or initiation, as well as by various other rites of passage.

Third, sacredness implies sanity and safety. While the mundane world may often laugh and call us crazy, there is nothing saner than realizing there's more to life than we normally see. There is nothing saner than admitting that we do not know it all and that, in fact, all religions may be partly right and partly wrong. There's nothing saner than taking control in your physical, spiritual, mental, and ethical life, keeping caution in your back pocket. Why caution? Because not every person or group in this world has your best interests at heart. In fact, the world as a whole can be relatively precarious. Safety first (as mom used to say) seems prudent.

You are responsible for the sacredness of your life and what you make of it. If you dive into a pool before checking for water, you get what you deserve. That may sound cold, but many people have become wrapped up in experiential spirituality and then have been hurt because they didn't consider the long-term (for example, people have tried to become part of a coven or study group and have been rejected for pervious behaviors). There is a time to act, and a time to think. Becoming whole, healthy, happy spiritual beings won't happen in a day. It's a process that requires ongoing effort and maintenance, which is why sacredness doesn't imply perfection. Rather, it means we're a work in progress.

Psychic and Physical Self-Defense

Neo-Pagans as a whole often quote the Wiccan Rede, "Harm none," when discussing how we treat each other and the world. But what about safety in the world? In nature, don't animals protect their territory, sometimes violently? Soldiers who die in sincere service to their country get credit for dying in the service of life, but does that alleviate their culpability for the deaths they caused? How do we protect ourselves, others, and this planet if we remain spiritual or social pacifists? If you bring up these questions in any Neo-Pagan group you're going to have a lively conversation, perhaps a heated one.

Sacred means inviolable. If we sit back and just "take it" (or, using the Christian phrase, turn the other cheek) are we honoring our sacredness? Perhaps not. I remember hearing one young woman say that she was taught not to do any type of protective spell because it might harm someone, specifically when the negativity aimed at her bounced back to the sender. Some people consider that kind of teaching unforgivable because it feeds the victim mentality and implies that the individual sanctity is not worth defending.

Proactive psychic self-defense is a much better option. It's better to have defenses in motion as part of honoring the sacred self. For example, you might carry an amulet that only goes into action when the situation calls for protection. This is certainly not harming anyone by being present. Having such items and outlooks doesn't mean you're expecting trouble under every rock. It just means you recognize that life isn't always nice, gentle, or wholly safe. Forewarned is forearmed.

But what about those times when you know you're being (or have been) attacked? When someone breaks into your home brandishing a weapon, for example, should we sit idly by and say, "It's all good"? Is it "all good"? In Chapter 2 we talked about retribution in terms of balance. This applies to self-defense, too. When another harms us, our life's wheel (and theirs) gets out of balance. If you've ever tried to ride a bike when one of the rims is dented, you know the effect—you get a very bumpy ride over which you have little steering control. You have to fix that dent to get the bike rolling again.

This is not meant to advocate randomly going around and meting out your own version of justice. However, few people can, in good conscience, tell anyone to stand by and do nothing when they're being harmed. When the situation calls for action, it will be up to your inner God/dess to determine what the best, right action will be.

Personal Boundaries

What limits (if any) do you feel are appropriate in psychic and physical self-defense? Can you give an example of a situation where you feel it's not at all appropriate?

Suicide in the Natural Order of Things, Life Eventually Leads to Death of the Body

Suicide is mindful death; individuals sometimes choose to end their lives. Many Neo-Pagans feel the reasons for a person's choice are just as important in our consideration as the next logical question: if reincarnation exists, then is suicide or assisted death wrong?

The answer to that very difficult question may possibly be found in motivations. Is someone thinking suicidal thoughts due to depression, peer callousness, or as a way of acting out? These situations sometimes happen to young people who have not as yet fully activated the sacred self, and aren't sure how to cope with all they're feeling.

To avoid potentially tragic results, the feelings of people suffering from depression and other illnesses must be acknowledged and dealt with. This is where Neo-Pagan ideals counsel returning to the God-Self. Look, listen, and empower that personal sacredness. When a person who has lived a full life and faces death without dignity or a person who can no longer live what he or she considers a "quality" life are under consideration, the problem becomes that even we, who consider ourselves somewhat spiritually awake and aware, often dance around talking openly and honestly about death and our feelings. This isn't healthy or helpful for that person or us.

Let's demystify death. Let's start talking about what it means to us, to the people in our lives, to our community. Let's talk how we want to honor this rite of passage. Metaphysically, when there is no hope, when there is no real quality of life, there is no question that situation compromises the sacred self. Our responsibility to both the living and dying is to protect sacredness. To do so, inevitably, some will choose to value the sacredness of life (even a limited one) over death. Some will find their faith challenged, and experience the "dark night of the soul" from which they emerge with new perspectives. Some will embrace death as the inevitable balancing of their life's wheel, turning once more, and trust in the next incarnation to sort things out. All of these actions (or inactions) can be correct if we are walking our talk and staying connected to the God/dess within. Each situation and person is unique and needs to be treated accordingly.

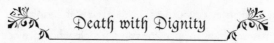

Should people have the right to end their life with dignity? If so, under what circumstances? Does this choice affect our karma? If you believe in living wills, have you prepared one for yourself?

The Sacredness of Family and Community

Can you see the God/dess in your mother, your father, your mate, and your children? Can you see the God/dess in your boss, a runway model, contestants of American Idol, and the annoying guy on the subway? All people are sacred, even the ones you don't like, and even the ones who are unethical and harmful. This realization puts the concept of family and community sacredness into a slightly different construct. How do we honor that sacredness, especially in people we feel aren't ethical, without compromising our other principles?

To help discuss this, change the words "family" and "community" to "tribe," as in the following statements:

‡ There is the tribe to which we are all born—the tribe of humankind.

‡ There is the tribe among which we live—our country or community.

‡ There is the intimate tribe that shapes our daily reality—our family.

Now, since a zygote doesn't really have a choice as to where it lands in this threefold tribal setup, it's quite likely dissatisfied with several individuals on all three levels of tribe, sometimes to the point of separation.

Although I am grateful for the tribe of humankind, there are days when I wouldn't mind being a cat or a tree. The cat gets fed, pampered, sleeps, eats, and plays. I could live with that. The tree? Well, you always know where they stand. Nevertheless, as a collection of thinking, reasoning, willful beings, humanity isn't such a bad group with which to be associated, especially considering our thirst for knowledge and betterment. That's a positive focus.

What about community? Let's look first at one of the larger pictures—our nation, whatever that may be for you. Our leaders will not always be perfect. Our rules and laws will not always be perfect. However, our path challenges us to stay involved, recognizing that even small efforts can have large effects (like voting). Not everyone was meant to be at the forefront of politics, but nearly all of us can do small things in our own backyards to illustrate those principles that we hold dear. For example, getting involved with a local soup kitchen would be a great way to serve your local community and be a positive representative of the magickal community. This honors our personal sacredness and embraces the larger community in a meaningful way.

As far as Neo-Pagan community goes, our individualism isn't always a healthy thing. In our grand efforts to promote individual vision, we have often come apart as a group and given in to "our way is the right way" thinking. If we are to honor the sacredness of all life, of families and community, we need to start acting more like a cohesive group. You may not always agree with or like everyone in that group. Even the ancient tribes didn't always get along with each other, and everyone has proverbial black sheep wandering around the edges of the community. Nevertheless, there is power in numbers. Our communal sanctity, longevity, and, by extension, safety depends on some level of cohesiveness—some basic ideas and beliefs that the world can see and quantify. That doesn't mean we have to have cookie cutter practices. It simply means focusing on those things we have in common, and putting those things forward to the world.

A good question to ponder personally and communally is this: how are we allowing our faith to bring us together rather than push us apart? This applies to family, too. All too often, matters of religion cause damage in families to the point where people don't speak for years.

A good illustration of this came up in a lecture I recently gave. A student who had a close relationship with her grandmother felt awkward about not sharing the fact that she was a Pagan with her grandmother. She feared the truth would hurt their relationship beyond repair. In this situation, the ethics of family sacredness brought silence, and left the girl wondering if her choice was the right one, if hiding such an important part of her life was hypocritical. Yet her response toward her grandmother was born from perfect love.

We have a comparatively short time in this world with our family. It is not hypocritical to simply avoid discussions about religion if those discussions would cause more harm than good. Faith is a personal matter that can be treated as confidentially as other personal data if we choose, especially when the situation warrants it. Silence and omission don't change our personal sacredness (who or what we truly are), nor will they change our actions other than helping us become more mindful of our words.

When magickal books aimed at a teen audience appeared in the market, some writers encouraged secrecy among teens and wrote that bucking the "system" (the parents) is good because faith is an individual's right. Some readers used these books and tools to purposefully cause a ruckus and get attention. This does not further the sacredness of the family and may have destroyed a bit of personal sacredness in the process.

My advice to teens is to honor their parents and the choices of their family until they become adults. While you can certainly try to explain your religious choices in hopes of acceptance or minimal tolerance, there are going to be cases where being out of the broom closet just won't work. These are the times to honor that family. If they have rules about Internet use, respect them. If they have rules about your books, respect them. If Neo-Paganism is truly your calling, it will remain a part of the sacred self until you're eighteen or older. In the meanwhile, you'll be doing something very spiritually positive: showing love and respect.

In short, if we consider our family a treasure, we will honor our family to the best of our ability. Now that doesn't mean staying in abusive situations (that wouldn't support the sacred self or inner God/dess), nor does it mean that you're always going to have a blissful, peaceful coexistence with these people (that's just not human nature). What it does mean is work—relationship maintenance, building communication skills, and finding ways to express our spiritual ethics even without words.

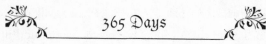
Come up with a minimum of ten ways in which you can viably support personal, family, and community sacredness over the next year. Set goals you can meet. Keep this list where you can see it and actively work toward those goals. Encourage others in your circle (family, coven, or whatever) to do likewise. At the end of the year, compare your notes and see the ways in which sacredness has blossomed.

Political Correctness

Inevitably, we come to a question of where to draw the PC line with our family and friends and with our communities. How much is it okay to hide without compromising our sacredness? How much should we fight against unhealthy trends? How often should we give into the status quo?

There is no question that we live in tumultuous times. The United States finds itself divided on many issues. Neo-Pagans as a whole have always been a bit outside the mainstream philosophically. How do we live in the world without our community or our family undermining all that we hold dear?

I have often joked that it's nearly impossible to be Pagan and PC at the same time. It may not be such a laughing matter. PCism has permeated our culture and one of the negative results is a mindset that ignores skills and experience in favor of balancing some unseen quota. While humankind cannot always be trusted to be fair and impartial, being PC does not seem to prevent prejudicial behavior. It may be dividing people even more.

Let's consider an example. Some women don't mind being called "ma'am" or "Mrs. ___." The first is intended as a polite term, and many women are actually thrilled at any type of common courtesy these days. "Mrs." is a correct (if old-fashioned) title, assuming that the woman has taken a married name. However, some feminists would be offended if you didn't call them by the more PC term "Ms." Others prefer that all gender-specific terms went away altogether. Such terms create a rift between those who use them and a global society that still needs certain terms for clear understanding (especially when we translate from one language to another).

When it comes to questions of political correctness, I would challenge us to consider where our energy is best applied. Don't jump on a bandwagon until you know who else is riding.

Daily Reality and Situational Ethics

In discussing the sacredness of life, it's important to touch ambiguous issues. How does a boss asking an employee to lie affect that person's sacredness, for example? If the individual refuses and loses the job, how does that affect the safety and well-being of his or her family? In making an ethical choice like this, the employee compromises her ethical self while at the same time she's faced with potentially compromising her family's stability. In this case, a possible way of dealing with this dilemma is to compromise the self temporarily . . . and immediately start looking for another job. It's not perfect, but it's a solution that a person could live with.

At times like this, we are reminded that our sacredness is connected to many other people and situations. We affect the social web, and it affects us. The more we live our sacredness to the best of our ability, the more we send our sacred energy outward. Like a wave on the ocean, it will eventually find its way back to the shore of our hearts.

Celestial Sacredness

Many of us believe that the time will come when humankind travels beyond our solar system and possibly encounters other life forms, which may or may not have intelligence that we can comprehend. While that day may be a long way off, thinking globally may come to mean thinking intergalactically. For example, is it okay for us to use space as our garbage dump? When we begin traveling to the stars, what about the pollution from rockets (not to mention the lessening of earth's resources in making that fuel)?

If we find living plants or animals, what becomes the ethical thing to do next? If we discover thoughtful beings, what will our place be in creating a new understanding of the universe, its structure, and how life's network functions on the grand scale? How will these beings describe deity, if at all? How will this new understanding affect our spirituality, our sense of sacredness, and our magick? These are all very big questions for a very big universe.

Commandment 7

The Judeo-Christian Seventh Commandment tells us,
Thou shalt not commit adultery.

Neo-Paganism says, All Acts of Love and Pleasure Are Sacred.

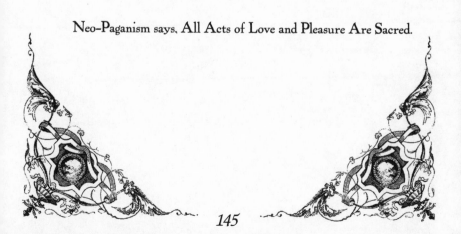

The Seeker moves, one step after the other, down life's roadway. Sometimes, the way is smooth, sometimes bumpy, sometimes chaotic, but no matter what, the Seekers aren't walking this path alone. All around, men and women, young and old, move ever toward the light on the horizon, toward the Monad with hope and vision as a guiding force. There is comfort in the company, a sense of belonging, of being kin of spirit. But what of the heart? It yearns for more substance, for contact, for intimacy; it seeks the Sacred We. Seekers begin to join their hands with others. Usually one, sometimes two, sometimes many . . . . Solitaries slowly, but surely, discover a new wholeness, a new unity, a new understanding with beings of a like mind and soul. As their hands unite, bodies dance, auras merge, and the Spirit of Love sings along joyfully.

All Acts of Love and Pleasure Are Sacred

It seems as if the Neo-Pagan community illustrates a wide variety of interpersonal relationships. This may happen because many Neo-Pagans see our emotions and our sexuality as integral parts of our sacred being. We embrace our passions, live and breathe them, just as we do any other aspect of our being. We believe that love cannot be contained in a box, that sexuality is a uniquely beautiful gift that was given to us in these bodies by the God/dess to enjoy and celebrate.

We see the symbolic or literal joining of God and Goddess in many Wiccan and other pagan rituals. Balance and equality of the sexes has had a profound impact on how we view our intimate interactions. Note, this does *not* mean that our religion is wholly tied up with sex. While we're long past the days of thinking of Pagan gatherings as orgies, we must still consider how our "out-of-the-box" outlooks affect issues from how we raise our children to choosing unique, and often misunderstood, lifestyles like polyamory in which a married couple may have other lovers to whom they open their hearts and lives on a long-term basis.

❧ Relationships in Review ❧

Make a list of the top ten relationships in your life. Next to each person's name, write how these people relate to each other or what common denominators they represent in terms of the kinds of people you enjoy having in and around your life. Afterward, make a special altar for these individuals where you can offer prayers for their ongoing well-being.

The Law of Love, Love and the Law

The Charge of the Goddess (attributed to Doreen Valiente) says, "All acts of love and pleasure are My rituals." This means acts of love and pleasure are sacred. Mundane law seldom shares this opinion, leaving us with many ethical and moral questions that aren't easily resolved. Where sacred and secular laws interact, who wins? Do we follow the law or risk prosecution because our hearts call us to a lifestyle of which the government doesn't approve? If we follow what we consider to be puritanical law, we deny self-fulfillment. If we risk doing what we prefer, that risk can prove very costly.

A fair number of Neo-Pagans seem to prefer taking the risk to denying the fundamentals of the sacred self and how they choose to love. We can try to suppress our feelings and hide them away in a secluded corner of our mind, but that's incredibly unhealthy.

Some individuals who feel they have no other choice but to live as society dictates later find themselves despondent. Others realize after months and years of pretending to fit a societal expectation that they've completely turned off their true passions. Others still find themselves lying to mates and family to cover up true feelings of attraction or other honest needs (being gay, bisexual, attracted to many lovers), for fear of hurting someone or being rejected altogether. It's no wonder some brave the risks of nonconformity. It would be wonderful if society changed so they didn't have to live in fear, but that day is a long way off.

The Polyamory Society cites many examples of how touchy this situation can get. Parents loosing children, even when evidence shows no abuse, is but one potential outcome people face every day. It's a fact that laws are slow to change, even with ongoing activism and education. We often forget that it's been less than a hundred years since women won the right to vote. The law has not kept up with social and scientific change, preferring political posturing. What does that mean for the gay couple wishing to wed? The extended family that wishes to embrace two wives or two husbands? The couple who chooses an open marriage? What does it mean for the next family legally assaulted by well-meaning in-laws who have issues with personal lifestyles or faiths? It means we need to use the legal resources we have effectively to protect all involved.

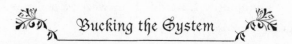 ### Bucking the System

If you had to choose between love and the law, what choice would you make? Why? How would you try to protect yourself and those you love from adverse affects that may be caused by a lifestyle choice?

The Big Box of Crayons: Bisexuality, Homosexuality, Transgenderism

All acts of consenting adult love and pleasure are sacred. That sounds pretty simple, but I suspect there are some people in the Neo-Pagan community who still struggle with their feelings about alternative lifestyles or feel awkward in their interactions with people openly living those lifestyles. Perhaps you just haven't shaken off the old preconceptions. Perhaps you simply can't wrap your mind around feeling "that way." Thankfully you're also in a community where you have an opportunity to reeducate yourself and turn your awkwardness feelings into something more positive.

How? First of all, realize that a person's sexuality is only one part of their whole beingness. To focus only on that small part is a disservice to the person. You'll never perceive that person's sacredness from a place of nonunderstanding. Unfortunately and ironically, in our puritanical society, sex is in front of us all the time. It's not surprising that we often make instant judgment calls based on what we perceive of another's sexual preferences.

There are moments when our misconceptions and perceptions came home in a bold way. Say a woman suddenly discovers she finds other women attractive after a lifetime of heterosexuality. That woman might not know how to act or feel, but she does have a solution available to her. She can seek out insights from known, trusted people in the lesbian or bisexual community within the Neo-Pagan community. She can talk to these women or read their books and try to find answers for herself.

As for the ethics of alternative lifestyles, from our foundational Neo-Pagan "commandments" (in the figurative sense) there is no reason to keep people from loving as their heart leads them, though within the boundaries of what is sensible, honest, and consensual. Celebrating the Spirit of Love means that we must allow for love's diversity, even as we allow for our spiritual diversity.

The Great Rite and Other Sex

Before going further into our consideration of the Great Rite and how it's viewed in the context of sacred loving, it's important to define what's what. In Wicca and Neo-Paganism there are very important differences between sex magick and enacting the Great Rite. Each has a distinct purpose, and to avoid misunderstanding it's good to have a functional understanding of each.

The Great Rite

The Great Rite is a ritual in which a man (priest) and woman (priestess) aspect the god and goddess, respectively. During the ritual, they perform literal or symbolic intercourse to represent the union of masculine and feminine energy. This energy is the basis of all existence and life in whatever form—human, natural, cosmic, etc. This rite is done (privately or communally) in sacred space with this specific intention, and the energy raised can either be directed toward that intention (often an urgent need) or honored, revered, and celebrated for what it is.

The symbolic Great Rite uses an athame (ritual dagger) inserted point down in a chalice. The dagger represents the male energies, the cup, the female energies. This symbolic approach can be used by two men or two women instead of the physical act. While two men or women could have intercourse with intent, the ability to create life does not exist in that combination, and thus we offer the alternative symbolism.

Sex Magick

Sex magick is defined as raising energy through a connection to sex and can be performed by interacting with another, others, or by yourself. It can include physical stimulation but can also be achieved through guided meditation and the evocation of that specific erotic energy from yourself or the cosmos around you.

We raise power with sex magick just like we raise any other kind of energy that we gather and direct in other types of workings, except that the vibration is very different. The feeling is comparable to an orgasm, and one can achieve an orgasmic sensation by simply thinking about it and reaching out with your imagination, and releasing yourself to that vision, just as you do in other magick. Most of us have just forgotten how and that this sexual energy is always in us.

Note that sex magick has no stipulation of man/woman, woman/woman, man/man, or even having to have more than one person. It also does not require that the practitioner(s) invoke any deity. However, the basic process for raising energy through sex magick is the same as the Great Rite (whether enacted physically or symbolically).

While the concept of a sacred sex might surprise you, it's not a new idea. In ancient Mesopotamia and Chaldea, for example, certain sexual services were regarded as a sacred profession, often connected with a specific temple. A person would come with an offering, request services, and then return home feeling blessed by a divine helpmate. A personal study of the Albanians, Syrians,

Babylonians, and Canaanites reveals that such services were performed by both males and females.

The Great Rite is a ritualistic union between god, goddess, and humankind. Wiccans and other Neo-Pagans typically reserve the Great Rite for very special occasions. Marriage is an obvious one, where the Great Rite cements and celebrates the couple's union and energizes the couple for fertility if they so choose. Other times, the ritual is enacted during times of great need, be it personal, communal, or global. Symbolically, it's also suited to the goal of abundance, prosperity, growth, etc.

It should be mentioned that not all covens "approve" of the Great Rite or sex magick in anything other than symbolic form. Because we still live in the United States, it's not that unusual for puritanical opinions to periodically infiltrate our beliefs. We also have people among us who have suffered abusive situations or who have very honest hang-ups about their sexuality that have yet to heal. Because of this, choosing to enact the Great Rite physically in a group setting could dramatically affect your relationships, and not always positively. We should use gentleness, discretion, and remain sensitive to this possibility.

I must stress that the Great Rite and sex magick are not having sex for pleasure, but for a defined purpose. They are not a free-for-all, an orgy, nor just for fun. The energy of loving or the symbolism of love creates a live magickal spark that is directed toward its goal. Because of the power of this rite and the invocation of divine powers, it's ethically unwise to undertake the Great Rite physically or symbolically without serious thought as to your motivations and the utmost respect for everyone participating in the ritual.

How to Enact the Great Rite

If you decide that your situation warrants it (and this should be a well-considered decision), and you wish to move forward and enact the Great Rite physically or symbolically as an expression of sacred sexuality, the next step is making preparations and choosing the right people. You need to be certain the other person or persons are comfortable with performing the physical act of the Great Rite, invoking deity, and engaging in sacred physical or symbolic expressions (such as placing an athame point down into a chalice) that will be used to raise energy.

Typically, it's best to work with two people or a small group of people that know and trust each other completely. Everyone needs to have a level of comfort with not only each other but also with the level of intimacy. Even a symbolic Great Rite can feel very intimate, and when it is undertaken with proper focus and intention, the energy it raises is just as powerful as the actual physical act.

Exercise your best judgment and listen carefully to your inner God/dess. Do not invite anyone you feel isn't prepared for this type of rite, regardless of your relationship with that person as a friend or teacher. Human nature finds us sometimes agreeing to things because we don't want to hurt a person's feelings. Unfortunately, if a person is not ready, the overall effect of the Great Rite is anything but positive and may instead create fear or misunderstanding. Note that enacting this rite is truly a sacred responsibility and remember: harm none.

Once you've decided on who will be present, create an environment that's comfortable for those participating. If you've chosen the physical rite, create a special, private area for it. A curtain or a nearby, separate room are two options.

Next, sit down with everyone and set up very specific guidelines, reviewing them before you put up the wards for the sacred space. Everyone should know that they have the option, at any time, to politely bow out if something starts feeling wrong, or that they can change the ritual slightly before its enactment to allow for more personal comfort. Besides this groundwork, there are a variety of ways to prepare all participants mentally, physically, spiritually, and emotionally for what's about to take place. For example, before the ritual, you can consider having each person create and charge something that will be used during the rite itself, such as incense, oils, beverages, etc. When these items are on the altar at the time of the actual working, they act as a trigger to bring the maker into harmony with the ritual intent and the rest of the group.

On the day of the event, ritual bathing and anointing can also help put people in the right frame of mind. These actions encourage the transition from the mundane to the magickal and also motivate participants to begin thinking of themselves and others as sacred beings. Preparation is doubly important for those acting as god and goddess during the rite. That couple not only has to overcome the mundane but also give themselves over to the divine. The other participants can treat the couple, or the couple can pamper each other in a style befitting the divine. The roles of god and goddess are typically enacted by the priest and priestess or another mutually consenting and well-trained couple.

Once everything and everyone is ready, the next step is creating sacred space. Nearly every tradition has its own way of honoring the four elements and asking for protection. I encourage you to find words that reflect your goals and the intimate nature of the working. You may wish to start the invocation in the south (to honor the fires of passion), and then dismiss starting in the west (to cool the fires, and honor our emotions). Here's an example that you should modify appropriately for the intimate nature of your ritual, and your goals:

> Powers of the South, of fire and passion,
> Come and watch over this sacred space.
> Inspire us with your sparks; ignite our spirits with
> Light and pure intention.
> Powers of the West, of water and emotion,
> Come watch over this sacred space.
> Inspire us with insight; wash us with wisdom and
> Clarity.
> Powers of the North, of earth and growth,
> Come watch over this sacred space.
> Inspire us with foundations, give our magick rich
> Soil in which to grow.
> Powers of the East, of air and communication,
> Come watch over this sacred space.
> Inspire us with transformation, move among us
> With the breath of life.
> So be it.

Note that you may wish to light candles or have other symbolic items placed around the loving space to set the tone and mood. At this juncture, I suggest everyone begin breathing together. Chanting is also very helpful (so long as the chosen words have meaning suited to this event). I have read a variety of "callings" or "drawings" for the divine, but because of the intimacy of this moment, I recommend the priest and priestess speak words that express their minds, hearts, and bodies with similar realness, respect, and resolve. As the energy of the divine fills each participant, the energy in the room will shift dramatically. The couple can indicate completion with the calling by simply stating, "I am God," or, "I am Goddess," followed by some type of show of willing trust such as, "And so we unite," spoken in unison.

This is when the physical or symbolic loving begins (calling the quarters, setting the space, getting everyone prepared, etc.). If there are other participants, they should focus on sending energy to the priest and priestess through visualization or a chant that slowly increases in volume and speed. The couple should continue to focus on the goal (where they want the energy of the ritual directed) and allow the cone of power to naturally grow. If this is a physical union, the energy is released at their climax; otherwise, it is released when the priest and priestess feel that the cone of power has peaked.

I recommend a pause toward the end of the ritual so that those who wish to do so can accept fertile energies into themselves and think about what this experience means in their own sacred sexuality. You should also allow time after opening the circle to discuss everyone's reactions, what they felt, when they felt it, anything special or unique.

While this sounds complex, it's also the most natural thing in the universe. These people are symbolically or physically expressing the human spiritual nature in the physical world (as above, so below!) in a sacred way. They are also honoring their connection to the God/dess within and without.

Do you foresee situations in which you might enact the Great Rite? Would you do it literally or symbolically? Why? Take the time to work on a ritual based on your choice and put it in your Book of Shadows for use when needed.

What Acts of Love Are Not Sacred?

While everything we do can be sacred, not everything we do is automatically sacred by virtue of the fact that we're spiritual beings. There are legitimate differences in our value judgments on issues like sex magick. I believe the ideas set forth in this book provide solid ground on which to consider our thoughts and actions (or those of others) by some common measure. The basis of that measure includes not only the will driving the action (was the inner God/dess at the helm?) but also the results of the action ("an' it harm none"). In the end, we may not always arrive at the same answers, but what we learn of ourselves, others, and the world in the process is well worth the time to try.

8 Commandment

The Judeo-Christian Eighth Commandment says,
Thou shalt not steal.

Neo-Pagans believe, Whatever you send out returns threefold.

The Seeker is not immune to stumbling; he or she sometimes loses site of the goal, or the road by which they walk. The lines of what is good and honorable and just get blurred amidst life's very real harshness. That gray dust kicked up by adversity, cruelty, injustice, and other societal ills hovers in the air and obscures spiritual vision. Where do we go? What do we do? In whom and what do we trust? Is this some type of challenge to overcome? Perhaps. The concrete jungle looms overhead, while the Spirit of Selfishness seeks to win the number game instead of striving for quality. All around the sides of the road, the mundane world screams in the Seeker's ear and pummels his or her eyes with unhealthy images. Meanwhile, the Seeker's god-self whispers tenaciously within, "Don't lose hope. Good will win out. Do what is right . . . listen, trust, and follow the light."

The light seems so dim . . . but it's there! It's reachable, and once the Seeker takes hold of that spark again, the fires can slowly grow until they burn brightly. Random acts of love and kindness replace despondency, and the web of goodness begins to stretch out once more to touch the one, the many, or the world.

The Threefold Law

"Do unto others." "What goes around, comes around." Sound familiar? That's because some sort of balance in the universe is implied in many of the world's religions and philosophies. We may not see the balance now, but eventually it will come.

Most people practicing a metaphysical lifestyle believe in some form of karma (or system of checks and balances). This system of balances applies not only to our magick, however, but also to our thoughts and behavior. On a simple level, we can see it with a person who tends to be cynical. Such people seem to have a never-ending list of issues with which to cope. That's because they're focusing on negativity, sending out negativity, and getting it back in spades. It is the law of "like attracts like" on a personal level.

Similarly, when a person begins to think more positively, they act more positively, and usually it's not long thereafter that things improve. Sure, part of this is just having a better outlook. When you're thinking positively, it's less likely that you'll see gloom and doom resulting from a tiny bump in the road. You're also more likely to try to find solutions because you're not caught in negative energies that often leave people impotent, frozen, and stagnant. The purpose of this chapter, therefore, is not only to consider the significance of the threefold law from all perspectives (including when good intentions are simply not enough) but also to think about our ideas about "goodness" and how they effect the Law of Three.

Three's a Charm

Before we specifically talk about the ethical considerations behind the threefold law, it may be valuable to deliberate whether our understanding of this concept is somewhat flawed at the outset. While the idea that all the "good stuff" we send out in this life will return to us three times is certainly pleasant and motivational, the law of symmetry doesn't allow for geometric progression.

Note that Newton's Third Law states, "For every action, there is an equal and opposite reaction." It doesn't say we'll get more or less, just "equal." When we say something will come back threefold, therefore, we're giving spiritual novices the hope of grand rewards, when a much smaller payout is more likely, even if we're only playing the averages. This can lead to some serious disappointment and disillusionment even among more adept seekers, which might be best stated in the age-old question: why do bad things happen to good people?

Philosophically speaking, we know that doing the "right" thing isn't supposed to be for the reward. However, the fact that we quote the three-fold law regularly as a Western representation of karma indicates that some type of reward is expected for extending good energy. Newton's law seems to support the idea of a balanced feedback loop, but it does not imply the threefold "add on." So where did we get this threefold return idea? Should we continue clinging to it?

Let's begin by looking at the lore surrounding the number three. People have long felt that there could not be two without three (that coupling naturally inspires growth—be it a group or a family), which is why we see trinities in various divine myths (two parts needing a third for balance, like a table with only two legs needing a third for stability). You can look in any book of numerology and find meanings for three. Think of common sayings like "good things come in three" or "three's a charm." Such sayings and beliefs surrounding this number appear in mythology, philosophy, and global lore, including:

- ‡ Greco-Roman mythology speaks of the three Moirae and three Graces (who play a role in human fortune and destiny).

- ‡ Celtic mythology tells us that oak, ash, and thorn are three sacred trees in which fairies live.

- ‡ In divination, when dice were tossed, three of the same number was regarded as a most fortuitous sign.

- ‡ Plato theorized that there were three great principles: matter, idea, and deity.

Today, we continue to talk routinely about a variety of triune concepts such as body-mind-spirit, past-present-future, thought-word-deed, and art-science-religion. Three, it seems, is truly a magick number.

✝ The Threefold Law may be an adapted remnant from Christian philosophy, the idea of reward or punishment, but on a more immediate and self-responsible level. To illustrate, how we handle our mistakes may have an impact now, and we can't merely seek forgiveness for those errors but also seek to *fix them*.

✝ Earlier magickal practitioners may have devised the law thinking to keep initiates from getting themselves in trouble. In this case, the three-fold law would have been considered information for the initiated only, not something to openly discuss. Bear in mind when considering this option that for a while in history, people thought there was a limited supply of magickal energy on which to draw. Therefore, it was prudent to keep certain secrets so the power was there when the magus most needed it.

✝ Early Wiccan practitioners (the 1960s, 1970s) may have used this concept in their PR/publicity to allay some of the fear and negativity surrounding magickal practices. People like Aleister Crowley were very colorful characters and prone to theatrical flair, so having something in place to ease trepidation makes sense. However, if this proves to be the case, we still can't know for certain whether or not these practitioners truly believed what they were saying.

✝ The law is a metaphoric adaptation of Newtonian philosophy (energy cannot be created or destroyed). In this instance, rather than being one dimensional, the Law of Return affects our body, mind, and spirit equally (thereby giving us three levels across which energy vibrates).

✝ The Threefold Law is an allegory for the way energy moves and responds and was never intended to be taken literally. If that's the case, we can probably thank the Gardnerian movement of the 1940s and '50s for establishing the basic notion, expressed poetically as, "Mind the Threefold Law you should, Three times bad and three times good." While no one is certain who first penned this, it has remained a cornerstone in many Wiccan practices.

The allegorical approach allows us to consider the second Newtonian law in our review (an object in motion tends to stay in motion until acted upon by an outside force). This would mean that any negative or positive energy we put out would keep moving and affecting the originator until it's somehow "acted upon" again. That ongoing influence, depending on how long it lasts, could add up to our threefold return. However, this doesn't account for those times when the energy is redirected, grounded, etc.

My theory is that the Threefold Law is an evolutionary blend of all of the foregoing. Since magick must work within natural law, then we're off the mark with the idea of a threefold return. If the Threefold Law is valid, however, then items 4 and 6 in the list provide the most logical foundation. How much we "get out" of our magick should not be the driving force for doing what is "good" and "right." But who exactly among us is qualified to measure, without prejudice or agenda, what is truly good or truly bad?

Can you remember any instances in your life where the number three seemed to be actively working for you? What symbolism regarding three did you get out of those experiences? Do you feel that three is, indeed, a charm? Why or why not?

Are You a Good Witch or a Bad Witch?

The terrifying archetype of the evil old hag rose out of several sources, including the medieval Christian Church, which was seeking to nullify women and hearth magick. The witch came to represent our hidden lusts, fears, uncertainties, and sins. It also neatly supported a misogynistic worldview.

This doesn't mean that there aren't "bad" people practicing magick or that some people haven't used magick for malicious reasons. There are bad people in all religions, as well as individuals who misuse any knowledge they're given. Neo-Pagans certainly aren't immune to the dark side of human nature. However, I think it's important to know where images like the "wicked witch" originated, especially when we're discussing internal philosophies and making judgment calls on the state of another's soul.

The "Bad" Witch

First, let's consider the "bad" witch in terms of what lessons the archetype teaches:

✝ **The "bad" witch never seems to be afraid of her powers, nor does she question them.** This implies a rather casual acceptance of magickal gifts as natural and readily available once mastered. What would our lives be like if we simply trusted in our spiritual nature as fully as she does?

✝ **The "bad" witch rarely hesitates to use magick to improve her fate.** She sees her magical abilities as a birthright and sees herself as wholly worthy of what those attributes bring. In this, we are reminded that the human ego serves a very real purpose. We must know and honor ourselves if we hope for any type of positive result from our workings (*as within, so without*). More importantly, we have to use our magickal methods and ideals if we ever expect either to impact our realities.

✝ **The "bad" witch laughs—rather, cackles—in the face of adversity.** You won't find this lady whining and wringing her hands over a poorly dealt hand. Instead, she sharpens her nails and her wits and tries another angle, flying off to that task fully anticipating success. Now, that's confidence!

✝ **The "bad" witch speaks strongly of the way we as a species perceive power.** Why must a woman's strength, confidence, and conviction be hidden behind old age and/or a displeasing visage? Because anything else would threaten the status quo. I'm pretty sure that if *The Wizard of Oz* were rewritten today, we'd discover that Dorothy was a young upstart, intent on taking over the wicked-witch's business deals. By the way, this new-improved wicked witch would wear a three-piece suit, carry a brief case, and ride a Hoover!

The archetype of the bad witch does have its darker side, the side that embodies energies that most modern witches strive to avoid. In the "what goes around, comes around" scenario, dark magick, while it may be successful, cannot only swing back to bite the user but it also negatively affects the user's aura in definable ways. To use the analogy of a radio, unless you're completely tuned to be evil and nasty, that type of energy is going to create static in and around your life, just if you tried to force an AM signal through an FM channel. Dion Fortune explains this very well in *Psychic Self-Defense*:

> One of the most effective, and also one of the most widely practiced methods of occult defense is to refuse to react to an attack, neither accepting nor neutralizing the forces projected against one, and thus turning them back on their sender. We must never overlook the fact that a so-called occult attack may be evil thought-forms returning home to roost.

Someone wielding negative magick will eventually see that figurative "wheel" turn around and come back to himself or herself. That alone becomes a pretty nasty prospect. Next, consider the kind of feelings someone would have to put into baneful magick. What sort of memories would they have to evoke? What kind of energies would that person call to himself or herself? If you stand too close to that type of energy, or stand in the wrong place at the wrong time, just as surely as if you were standing too close to a raging fire, you're going to get hurt.

Many people cannot figure out why anyone would choose to go to the "dark side" after weighing the consequences. It seems obvious that any sensible practitioner would carefully avoid baneful magick.

However, there *is* an allure in dark magick, one that comes from wielding power without worrying about tomorrow . . . one that comes from the spirit of selfishness that grows fatter the more it gets fed. Make no mistake. We all walk a very fine line between good and bad, but the farther over that line we go in either direction, the harder it becomes to distinguish where it was originally.

Additionally, there is also a chance that some people were pushed into what could be considered "dark" magick out of desperation (such as feeling helpless when a loved one got hurt, and running out of mundane ways to try and help). Or people may do a good thing for a bad reason. It's a good thing to want to help others, but sometimes that turns into enabling. There are moments in every person's life when they're pressed to a wall, when they feel as if there are no good choices, or when they feel the need to fight back. Most of us have faced that moment of truth. What then? No one wants the Threefold Law to hit with full force with negative energy.

Our first stop could be to research old magickal texts. As you do, it won't take you long to discover that our ancestors used magick for things that might be considered ethically "iffy" today, from curses born out of fear and suspicion to spells aimed at getting even with a foe, likely due to the severity of living conditions.

The Wicked Witch Within

What attributes do you like about the "bad" witch? What aspects of her personality would you wish to integrate into yourself? And why do you need them? What attributes of the "bad" witch do you feel are truly "bad" (negative, unproductive, unhealthy, abusive, or manipulative)? Do you see any of these dark spots in your own soul that need cleansing?

The "Good" Witch

Thanks to the magic of movies, it's nearly impossible to separate the Good Witch archetype from Glinda in *The Wizard of Oz*. This type of witch waves a rose-colored wand and all the problems of the world float neatly away. She smiles a disarmingly innocent smile and trusts wholeheartedly that all of the world's ills will eventually fix themselves through the law of return.

Alternatively, you have Samantha from the television series *Bewitched*, refusing to use her powers except in emergencies, and only if they're used for "good." What made the "good witch" archetype work in the popular mind forty years ago was the fact that she didn't interfere and hesitated to wield her power, effectively immobilizing any sense of threat. She wasn't trying to be special; she wanted to be normal.

For the modern Neo-Pagan, Wiccan, or Witch, this creates an odd challenge. What is truly "bad" or "good" about the "good witch?" Some beginners' books on Wicca give the roundabout impression that a spiritually proficient life is nearly idyllic. It is almost as if the writer is saying, "If your life isn't like this everyday, you're doing something wrong." Meanwhile, it's hard not to think, "Hey, you! Your life isn't like this either!" Most people's lives aren't the material from which Hallmark cards are made.

Why do we create mundane or magickal yardsticks up to which no one can possibly measure? That is the true danger in the "good" witch; she's got a very tough, if not impossible, act to follow. None of us are completely enlightened, or we wouldn't still be here, going through another round of life lessons.

Meanwhile, the "good" witch archetype stands there, looking pristine, never shaken, always grinning as if there's not a care in the world. How many of us can say we ever look like that? The Good witch archetype externally gives the impression that perfection just comes naturally (except perhaps for the glitter). But real witches know better. We know that true magick takes more than a bucket of fairy dust to manifest.

Another concern I have with the "good" witch is the all-too-simple instructions she gives. "Follow the Yellow Brick Road . . . don't stray from the road . . . .

Additionally, in her unshakable optimism, the "good" witch can often be taken quite unaware by life's significant ups and downs (the turning wheel). It's great to expect the best, to put energy toward good things. That's part of feeding the Law of Return. However, there must always be a rational balance point—a place to which you return to regroup when the rug gets pulled out from under your broom. No witch worth her wand would be caught dead tripped up on a floor with tusseled hair and a wrinkled robe, but that's exactly what can happen if the good witch gets too out of touch with reality. Sometimes things go wrong, but when that happens, just pick up your broom, clean up, laugh, regroup, and get on with it. Maybe that is exactly why Glinda's mantra for Dorothy was, "there's no place like home." Perhaps Kansas was Dorothy's regrouping point once she got some perspective.

So what is the flip side of the good witch archetype? Is there something in her to which we should aspire? We all know that doing good things feels good, and that feeling good creates a kind of instant reward. However, the good witch's naïve trust says, "It's all good," (even when it's not). And it's also not the fluffy-bunny-crystal-jockey-weekend Wiccan image that smacks of superficiality instead of quality inner transformation.

The Good Witch says:

Let's tackle this from a different angle. From what I can see, the best lessons the good witch embodies are:

‡ A positive outlook can be a powerful ally.

‡ Some problems are not as big as they seem (or as big as we make them).

‡ There's wisdom not only in knowing when to act but also in when to remain still.

‡ You really do get more flies with honey than vinegar.

These philosophies, used effectively, can empower the practitioner. When your outlook is upbeat, the "as within, so without" rule affirms that things will, eventually, turn around and balance out. Optimism and determination also allows magick to flow much more smoothly at the right best moment. After all, Dorothy wasn't really ready to go home to Kansas when she first met Glinda; there were important lessons she had to learn. Dorothy would have never internalized those lessons if Glinda had simply handed her an easy out, no matter how contrived the solution. Don't take this story as implying that the good witch doesn't know how to influence people, too; she just goes about it differently.

The positive perspective, when kept in balance, also gives us some emotional distance so we can see what is truly a mountain and what is only a molehill. This isn't a picture-perfect outlook that only recognizes the positive. Rather, it's one that tries to find a silver lining, an alternative, or a solution. It's a can-do attitude. When you find that you've been looking at the same old wall too long, the good witch says, "Step away, look around, and find the path to circumvent that blockage."

And what of action versus inaction? We all have to learn how and when to pick our battles. There are some things that are none of our business. Other things involve us, but it's not really our place to "fix" the situation. Other situations require thought before action to determine the right, best thing. In any case, the good witch reminds us to stop and think for a moment, to check our motivations, and then determine what course of action to take, if any.

Finally, being able to communicate through word or deed in a positive or proactive way, especially in the face of difficulty, gains far more willing support from others than the "poor me" attitude ever will. There's nothing that's more of a turnoff than someone stuck in pouting mode and not doing anything to change their fate. I know I don't enjoy hanging out with people whose lives get out of whack at the first sign of a hangnail.

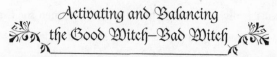

Activating and Balancing the Good Witch–Bad Witch

Come up with three mundane ways and three magickal ways to accent the positive attributes of the good witch within your self. Put them into practice regularly. Repeat this activity with three attributes of the bad witch that you perceive as helpful in your reality. Make notes of your experiences.

Right Thing/Wrong Reason; Wrong Thing/Right Reason

Remaining aware of individual acts and their potential consequences is part of a complex picture. We also have to ponder our behavior patterns, what drives us, what we choose to justify, what we ignore, what ticks us off, what shuts us down. Once we isolate those triggers, it also helps to sort out the what, when, and why of action or inaction. This is what the Buddhists call right mindfulness and concentration: an awareness and attentiveness that allows us to calmly see the true order of things (action/reaction) and the true nature of things (what really is a problem, what is something to which we should give our energy, etc.).

The study of ethics boils down to the study of right and wrong. In any case, we are seeking to figure out what to do in any given situation, to know what is socially or spiritually acceptable and expected, to act upon what we personally value. Now, not all choices are traumatic—we make ethical choices every day. But how do we end up doing the right thing for the wrong reason, or vise versa? It goes back to exactly where we're placing our awareness and attentiveness.

Let's look at it this way:

✝ If it makes me happy, it's right, versus if it works, it's right.

✝ If it helps my friend, it's right, versus if it's fair, it's right.

In these two examples, a person is trying to find the right behavioral standard on which to base his actions. The first option in both examples is more egocentric, the second, more global. When a person chooses the first option, they may indeed make the right choice (one that works, one that's fair), but the reasoning isn't global. This gets us into the "ends justified by the means" kind of scenario. The energy generated from this type of magickal or spiritual choice may be positive, but it will have that underlying taint that's likely to create static.

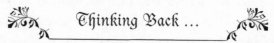

Thinking Back ...

Can you remember a time when you did the right thing for the wrong reason? What was the result? Have you ever done the wrong thing for the right reason? Of these two situations, which one worked out better? Why do you believe that result came about?

What about doing the wrong thing for the right reason? This happens sometimes in medical research. A physician or scientist discovers a link between item X and illness Y and jumps to take action to stop that connection. However, without knowing exactly under what specific circumstances the link occurs, they may end up worsening matters. The motivation is quite good and noble, but the results are anything but what was desired or intended.

A magickal example would be a banishing. We spoke about this previously in the section about "As Above, So Below." A witch discovers that something from their past is hindering spiritual growth, so they banish that thing, be it a feeling, experience, or person. The problem is they didn't consider how that specific part of self influences things in the physical, emotional, and mental realms, too. So, again, the results will likely be less than satisfactory unless they do a releasing ritual instead, which is a better option.

In all of these illustrations, there is definitely a balance somewhere, whether now, or later, within or without. This balance, in my opinion, is more appropriately called the Law of Attraction.

Law of Attraction

For a moment, let's assume that rather than the Law of Three, we are more accurately governed by a reciprocal Law of Attraction. This would mean that each person creates his or her own reality by those things to which they give energy, focus, and attention. For example, if you're in a difficult job situation, and constantly focus on how much you hate that situation you're never going to notice the good things, let alone opportunity's knock when it comes. We obsess about the negative, or alternatively, and perhaps more detrimentally, we concentrate on something that realistically may be out of our reach or never happen (such as winning a huge lottery).

Part of the problem begins in how we qualify our lives. If you say the word "abundance" to someone, most people immediately think of money, often followed immediately by additional thoughts of how much they *don't* have. However, with a more enlightened outlook, our minds should go to things like good friends, insightful advisors, a healthy body, etc. For example, person A says that she'd buy her father a car if she won the lottery. Meanwhile, she could get her current car in working order for far less or find a reasonably priced car with affordable payments. If you were to ask Ms. A why she does neither of these things, it is most likely because she worries over how much money would be left afterward rather than seeing a potential solution. Basically, with this perspective it will never matter how much you have. Enough will never be truly enough.

Now, the car example may sound terribly mundane, but the difference between "this is impossible" and "what can I do, what tools are available to me?" is huge no matter what the venue. When we stop focusing so much on what we don't have and turn our thoughts to what is available and possible, the solutions clarify. I believe that this technique can be applied to our spiritual pursuits. Don't cling to a negative reality. If you find you're not feeling motivated or aren't growing, don't shrug your shoulders and walk away. Apply some positive energy, get off your butt, and do something. Whether that energy returns once or three times doesn't matter. What matters is that you reclaimed your role as a cocreator of your destiny.

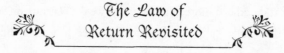

The Law of Return Revisited

How do you plan to change the way you think, speak, and act/react to feed the Law of Return, however you perceive it, in a positive way every day? How do you think this will manifest in your reality? How long will it take?

Of course, you may ask why your reality isn't exactly what you want. The answer is simpler than it seems. Every time we give thought to what we don't want, what worries us, what upsets us, what pushes us down or back, that is what, by the Law of Attraction, we're actually helping manifest. Society doesn't help a lot. Just collect a week's worth of newspapers and see how many uplifting articles you find—not a lot. This creates programming in our mind that undermines even the most positive thoughts with phrases like, "but what if . . . ," or "there's no way . . . ," etc. That fleeting negativity just washed away the positive drive that could have created success.

Proverbs 23:7 tells us that "as a man thinks in his heart, so is he." That's the Law of Return. The heart as an emotional center is figuratively the space from which our faith arises, or, in New Age terms, where our personal vibration lies. The problem for many of us is that some of our self-limiting vibrations are so ingrained that we don't even recognize them until someone or something brings them into focus.

For me, and for many others in the Neo-Pagan community, it manifests as the "I'm sorry" bug. Many people apologize for everything, including things over which they have no control. Too much apologizing can be a symptom of a much deeper issue: personal image and the ability to think of ourself as "good enough" or "worthy."

If it weren't complicated enough that each of us is creating (and uncreating) our reality each moment of every day, so is everyone else. People influence each other's thoughts and actions, knowingly or unknowingly. This interaction and the energy it produces can be chaotic, to say the least, even without a three-fold return. This is why I believe that sometimes bad things just happen, and they have nothing to do with karma, nothing to do with the Law of Return. Rather, it is merely an odd interaction of vibrations needing an outlet. It's only a theory—your mileage may vary!

9 Commandment

The Judeo-Christian Ninth Commandment says:
Thou shalt not bear false witness against thy neighbour.

Neo-Paganism says, Love is the law, love under will (a phrase
originally penned by Aleister Crowley and used regularly in
many different schools of Wicca).

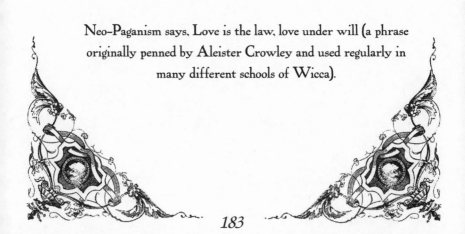

The world of a Seeker is filled with experiences, each of which drives a feeling, a thought, or an action. Not all are pleasant, sunny, welcoming . . . not all make the Seeker feel "good," let alone remotely spiritual. Yet, behind the throng of ongoing input there remains a low, deep, resonating drum sounding steadily. This is the rhythm of life, of the universe, of Self, of Soul, of Deity . . . it is the first note in the sonata of Love. What is this song's message?

At first, the rhythm drew Seekers to each other for kinship. Later, it encircled small groups of them for deep, abiding relationships. But the Spirit of Love is more than togetherness and romance. Love wells within each Seeker when we rejoice at the sunrise. It dances through our fingertips when we cuddle a treasured pet. It sings through our soul as we create majestic art or finish a bliss-driven project. It is part of each heartbeat and every breath we take.

Love is the smile that comes unbidden when we take the hand of a child and walk together on a sunny day. Love is the rainbow as it kisses the dew-laden grass and our eyes feast on that beauty. Love is the starlight stretching to embrace the world and give us something on which to hang a wish. Love has thousands of dimensions and sounds, facets and textures . . . . But most of all Love is a choice.

Love Is the Law,
Love Under Will

*L*ove and trust are rarely perfect. We are humans with limitations and failings, yet we strive for this perfection. Thus, we come to the point of discussing the importance of love and will, and that often-elusive heart-head balance necessary for walking a positive magickal path successfully.

There's balance in our path. The empowered seeker keeps his or her eyes on the horizon but knows well the way he or she walks. If we look too far forward, we're likely to stumble over the stone lying just before our feet. If we look down all the time, we may take the wrong fork in the road and miss our goals altogether. In short, there is a place, and indeed a need, for both reason and intuition in our practices. In the context of this chapter, love is the intuitive and will the reason.

Love Versus Will

Before breaking down this expression further, let's give pause to the question of whether love should be "under" will. The word "under" means:

- ✝ A state of being overwhelmed or burdened by

- ✝ Inferiority or subordination

- ✝ The current subject ("under discussion")

- ✝ Attested to (such as "under one's own hand)

- ✝ Represented by (under a coat of arms, under a flag)

Point by point, first love does not seem to be "overwhelmed" by will. If anything, love often overcomes common sense without much effort. It's possible, however, for love to be "burdened" by will. For example, sometimes, we fall in love with an ideal, or a group, only to discover later that one, the other, or both, simply aren't realistic or healthy. It is in this moment of awareness that love may give way to will; we must make a choice, even if it's painful.

Point two: Inferiority—this has a lot of negative to it. Neither love nor reason nor will are "better" or "worse" than the other except in how they are applied. Again, we come back to our actions and how they reflect our ideals and ethics. Some might say that love makes a person weak; being able to love (in all its forms), especially in the long-haul, however, takes great strength. Nonetheless, emotion alone is not enough to see a person through the most difficult times. Reason is a valuable companion in our struggles, one that helps us measure what we feel against what is real or possible!

What about subordination? This would indicate ranking or superiority, a concept that thus far seems lacking substantiation. Reason has given us much, but so has love in all its forms. To say one ranks higher than the other, in terms of human acclaim, would be very difficult to prove, let alone substantiate.

How about love "under discussion?" Now, this has potential, because when it comes to love we certainly do talk about it. In fact we talk about it a lot. We talk to our friends, our families. We read books and columns for the lovelorn. We watch informational programs about what makes for healthy relationships. We inwardly mull over what we feel or do not feel. Discourse with others and with ourselves (as within, so without) is important, but ultimately it's the inner discussion (thou art God/dess) that's most likely to win out, especially among a vision-driven group of Neo-Pagans.

Personally, I also have a favorable reaction to the idea of love being "attested to" by will. This supports the idea that love is a mindful choice. This could effectively work hand-in-hand with the next point, "representation." We choose to love, then we represent that love by our decisions and the actions and words that follow.

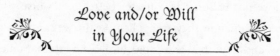

Love and/or Will in Your Life

If you had to choose between love or will, which do you think drives you more strongly? What is it about the aspect of self that gains control, and when does it happen? Who are those people, what are those things that you choose to love? Why?

What Is Love?

The greatest thinkers of all ages have tried to explain the spirit of love, so modern Neo-Pagans shouldn't feel bad if we're still trying to grasp what this emotion means in our spiritual and mundane lives. Before moving forward to talk more about love versus will, it's important that we have a sense of where our ideas about love originate. With that foundation in place, we can then make some soundly reasoned decisions when it comes to "perfect" love as it applies to our path.

Love's power has a long-standing written testament. As early as 2000 B.C., the Sumerians and Babylonians were writing love epics. This was followed by the Egyptian love poetry of B.C.E. 1300, Chinese love songs in 1000 B.C., and philosophical papers written by people as diverse as Plato and Santayana (a principal figure in American philosophy). With all these great minds pondering love, it's not surprising that we discover a similar diversity of historical opinion as to what does (or does not) constitute love.

From a Greco-Roman perspective, love was a double-edged sword. The happiness experienced when one is in love knows no bounds, but that same love can take over all reason. Effectively, the lover becomes "possessed" by Love's spirit. Additionally, the sadness of love lost is likened to a pain beyond compare. This dichotomy with regard to love is one we certainly still see today, and it's one that shows itself in a wide variety of cultures.

The Greeks also illustrated love as being a power that comes from Eros and Aphrodite and other gods and goddesses. These beings provided mortals with whole new dimensions of feeling, be it outright passion or intense romance. It is from this era that we get the image of Cupid striking humans with love's arrow, inspiring an intense love that could not be understood or shaken.

Amorous Archetype

Choose any person living, dead, or fictitious, who, to you, best represents the Greek essence of love. Why did you choose this person? Do you see anything of this archetype in yourself?

Plato spoke of love as something that helps us complete ourselves. In effect, each person is looking for their "other half," the half that will complete them. The story goes that the first humans had two parts that could be any combination of masculine or feminine (male-male, male-female, female-female). These combinations were considered threatening to the gods, so they were divided, forever to seek out that other half. The fact that we still use the phrase "my other half" in talking about our mates speaks volumes to how strongly Plato's views influenced humankind. While seeking after another to make yourself "whole" certainly isn't the healthiest outlook, being aware of that potential motivation will help us discover a more realistic approach to perfect love.

What about romantic love? This concept arose in a variety of settings but is easily recognized with poets like Keats and Shelley (or if you're looking for the slightly darker side of romance, there's Wagner and Shakespeare). In either case, love's energy motivates the individual to be honorable and to treat the potential spouse like a treasure to be kept pure and safe. Romantic love focuses on the "chase" as a prelude to intimacy, and the happily-ever-after ending.

In the darker versions of these writings, that ending doesn't happen, which ties back into the earlier bittersweet Greek view.

Ever After

Rewrite the story of your life with an "ever-after" scenario for yourself. What from your past gave you the sense that this "ever-after" portrait was perfection? Did you ever do anything really silly or really wonderful in pursuit of that ideal? Do you have any regrets about that ideal or do you see it changing in the future? Finally, do you feel your "ever after" affected your spirituality in any way? If so, how?

On more lofty levels, we get messages that love is a divine attribute; not merely inspired by the gods, but an integral part of the godhead. This love is called *agape*, or perfected, righteous, good, nonsexual, love. There are positive things about this concept for Neo-Pagans who are trying to stay in touch with the God/dess-self (within and without). It means that somewhere in our spirit there is a pattern of perfected love. However, we should remain mindful that activating perfected love every moment is something very few humans ever achieve, meaning the goal is marvelous but the reality isn't always that beautiful.

Tied into the divine love, we see a spiritual sense of love enter human thoughts. Courtly love tries to separate romance and sex. So does *agape*. Here, the purest love overcomes the struggle against the animalistic instincts (the drive to reproduce). One loves because it is the right, best thing to do, not as a means to an end. This is a relatively common model of the love among close friends and family; the spiritual love that gives because it chooses to, not because it seeks after physicality.

Counting the Ways

How do you love? How intense is your love? What separates casual appreciation from actual love?

With our brief review of historical and philosophical views of love out of the way, we can now begin to try to describe perfect love, and love in other forms, a little more firmly. For example, liking and caring about someone, and even feeling a level of attachment toward that person, are all part of love, but they're also part of liking and friendship. Each person draws a line that once you step over it, here is LOVE (kind of like X marking the spot). This is also true with spiritually oriented love. Now, to make things a bit more confusing there are different elements to love. There are:

‡ **A love that feels close affection and compassion, but does not feel any need or desire for sexual manifestation.** Compassion is born out of positive reinforcement, such as in a good friendship.

‡ **Passionate love.** Passion is physical and often depends on chemistry as much as intellectual or spiritual connection. While most of us would wish to have the best of both worlds in our long-term relationships, a study of human behavior shows that the "ideal" isn't often achieved, and even when it happens, may not last.

‡ **Playful love and pragmatic love.** The person who treats love as a game is often competitive in nature. The person

who approaches love very realistically is not likely to be overly romantic. Again, playfulness and realism have a place in intimate relationships, but finding the best balance between these two is usually healthier for lasting interactions.

Infatuation has very little true intimacy but tons of sexuality and attraction. An overly pragmatic relationship, meanwhile, lacks zest but offers plenty of devotion. A friendly love provides people with all the intimacy and commitment they need, but little passion. There are numerous situations where any of these combinations may be perfectly appropriate. A lot depends on what we want, what we need, what's appropriate, and where our goals lie. In the Neo-Pagan community, where we're striving for "perfect love and trust," one would think that intimacy and devotion would be the primary force. However, the pessimist in me says, hold on, there. Separate the ultimate ideal from reality.

Colors of Your Love

Gather crayons and a piece of paper. Think about a close friend. What color and texture would you assign to that feeling? Draw it. How about an aroma or a taste? Now, think about a family member you care for deeply. Answer the same questions and try to express those feelings visually. Finally, repeat this exercise when thinking about someone with whom you're intimate, and when thinking about someone with whom you share strong spiritual ties. Now, review your drawings. How do your responses help you better understand how you sort and designate your relationships? What do they say about your spiritual counterparts as friends and lovers?

Imperfect Love and Will

As with the other ethical guidelines in this book, the concepts of love and will, no matter their relationship to the individual and actions, are usually put on a pedestal. This is a very dangerous place to set such lofty ideals. Humans are imperfect beings, so our love and will are likewise imperfect. It's no wonder we so often find ourselves disappointed by the reality of our lives, communities, and world. Perfect love and will are very high bars to reach.

The fact that perfect love and trust are hard to achieve doesn't mean we shouldn't try. Most people think of the ideal love as being unconditional, and the ideal will as that which is well considered and focused. Think about that. Unconditional love means that no matter what someone does, you love him or her. No matter what type of person he or she is inside, you love perfectly. It's easy to see where the concept of unconditional love can and often does create a doormat mentality. Striving to love perfectly can leave us feeling like we have no options, no means of action, but for the one that seems to *not* love in that idealistic way.

Many people reading this are probably thinking about their families or other groups in which there are people you *love*, but may not *like* very much. This is certainly not a perfect love. It's a love that hesitates, and probably for good reason. Even so, the communal love-link (to other people, or whole groups) shouldn't be underestimated because we feel a strong responsibility to it.

Say you have a brother or sister that you looked up to as a child. As an adult, however, you find some of their attitudes and outlooks deplorable. This same sister or brother is having a hard time of things financially, in part because of his or her attitude. Do you help out? What does love demand? What does will counsel?

Love's immediate response is to say, "Sure I'll help." Will, however, steps in with other questions such as:

‡ Will this person learn anything if I help? (Will they change?)

‡ Am I enabling bad behavior by helping?

‡ Am I denying my personal sacredness and sense of ethics by helping?

These are the kinds of questions for which will (and wisdom) are/ is famous. It keeps nagging at you, even when love screams otherwise. It is good to at least heed the inquiry long enough to know you can face yourself in a mirror after you've made a choice.

With this example in mind, the best love may actually be a conditional love, a love that celebrates the best a person can be, even if they're not quite "there" yet. A love that is earned. A love that is a choice. The beauty of moving love into the realm of personal choice is that then it also becomes a personal responsibility. If you decide to love, be ready for all that goes with it.

It's also good to recognize that a person cannot fully give and receive love until he or she also loves the self with similar realism. Each of us is prone to error, but so long as we keep striving to be better human beings, we are worthy of love. This self-awareness-love and the bliss that follows are tied directly to eventually finding and fulfilling our destiny. When we love ourselves, when our confidence finds firm footing, we can walk toward the future without hesitation.

What about will? By definition, will is a mental faculty that helps us choose when to do or not do something, to determine those things within our power, to determine our purpose.

In terms of spiritual attunement and awareness, the will of the individual is supreme within the realm of that person's reality unless they choose to give that release, that will to a higher power. He or she becomes a complete participant in action, thought, words, etc., as well as in the accountability for each. In fact, the concept of love being represented by will charges each seeker with the task of focusing on those things of which they are capable, which, of course, changes as we grow and stretch in our spirit, and doing them wholeheartedly (with love). Will and love come from within and without, and motivate self-mastery.

 Perfecting Love and Will

Knowing that love and will are not perfect is part of being human. The God/dess within, however, has the capacity to help you strive to improve your human nature. What ways can you think of to help yourself begin perfecting love "realistically" instead of "idealistically"?

Trust, Love, and Will: A Difficult Trinity

In talking about love and will, it's nearly impossible to not also ponder trust and its role in our lives. Most individuals begin by thinking the best of others, even if we can't quite quantify what that "best" truly is. Likewise, most people want to be trusted and try to gain trust by saying what we mean, and following through in our actions. Trust is the core of meaningful relationships, including those in our community. But what exactly is trust?

Depending on the situation, trust may be a social coping mechanism. In fact, trust seems to be expected in some situations, and if a person refuses, they're given a negative label. Here, guilt is used to control or conform trust. I do not think that's what we intend when we say "perfect trust." Take a coven that requires you to do something that goes against your personal ethical code to remain a part. This plays upon people's insecurities; it's manipulative, plain and simple, and certainly doesn't honor the inner God/dess-self.

In other instances, trust reflects innocence or naiveté, perhaps because the individual is uninformed or immature. In this case, the trust may be impulsive or risky because no thought as to future consequences ever enters into that person's mind (such as getting married after only knowing someone a very short time). This commonly happens among the novices of the Craft who jump into situations because of overenthusiasm, even though they may realize they're not really ready for that step. This hardly seems like what we're trying to attain through perfect trust. We who have walked the path for a while should gently advise novices that there's no hurry in making important personal and spiritual choices. Give them options, ideas to consider, help them pause and truly think.

Trust is a good virtue, one we should strive for. Socially, however, trust comes into play in situations where we as yet have no foundation for confidence. For example, when you meet someone for the first time, you can't really predict behavior or how interactions will go (other than perhaps by an anticipated reaction based the group with whom you associate that person).

In either case, it's just wishful thinking until experience dictates otherwise. Consequently, trust implies giving, risking, and bonding. What happens, however, when the giving is one way, when the risk results in pain, or when the bond is betrayed? Do we simply say, "It's all good"? The answer should be no, but in my opinion among Neo-Pagans as a whole, there appears to be too much willingness to turn a blind eye toward, accept, and even enable hurtful behavior.

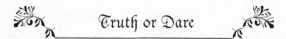

Truth or Dare

Can you think of a situation that you feel was unethical or dishonest and you avoided speaking up because everyone else seemed to accept or ignore it? How about watching someone repeatedly hurt others in the community because they don't think about the impact of their words and actions? What does the love-trust-will trinity require of you in these situations? When does it become your "job" to speak up, stand up, and act for change?

We Neo-Pagans like to think ourselves a sensitive lot, and for the most part we are. However, that doesn't mean wolves in sheep's clothing don't exist, nor does it mean everyone among us is adult enough to handle the difficulties of love-will-trust. It is healthy, and perhaps even necessary, that we allow ourselves to be disappointed, or even enraged, when a person's or group's behavior turns out to be ill-motivated or hurtful. However, it is not healthy or necessary to blame everyone for that person's or group's behavior in your future interactions with others. In other words, let's keep the blame where it belongs, that is, focused on those that do harm (and on ourselves if this is repeated behavior on our part).

Rebuilding trust becomes a matter of effort. Don't mistake forgiveness for trust; they're very different things. The idea of "forgive and forget" has flaws—your memory of that situation can provide the foundation for avoiding a similar problem in the future. Rather, consider "forgive and transform." In other words: fix it if you can, move on with new understanding if you cannot. Forgiveness can be given. Trust must be earned, and you have the right to expect that effort from people who want to be close to you for a season or a lifetime. And if you're the person who needs to regain trust, be prepared to put that effort forward honestly if the relationship or situation truly matters to you. It's vital that you communicate truthfully, be meticulous about doing what you say you will do, don't make excuses, and don't hide those things that you used to conceal.

Before going on to talk about trust-love-will and emotional responsibility, there's one point about trust that is vital to consider. Humans naturally interpret other people's words and actions by a personal measure. Family, culture, society, and personal experience all combine to create that measure. This means that our sense of who or what is trustworthy may get skewed. This occurs often in intimate relationships where one person speaks, and the other hears something different. Person A used words and phrases that make sense in his or her reality. Person B listened and interpreted those words according to his or her own spiritual and situational framework. The result is often a huge misunderstanding (even to the point of thinking Person A lied) that could hurt the spirit of trust. Please keep this potential problem in mind when sorting out your personal and spiritual trust-related matters.

Untangling Trust

What role do you feel trust should take in your spiritual life? How does this differ from mundane trust issues (if at all)? Can trust be perfected realistically? Are there times when another chance to retain trust should not be given?

Personal Emotional Responsibility

The topic of emotional responsibility fits in perfectly with our discussion of what we hear versus what a person meant and how that affects group dynamics. While we all have expectations regarding various social circumstances, the choice of how we interpret a person's words and actions is nearly always wholly our own. Say Person A declines an offer to go to a movie with you. We could interpret that as meaning they're busy, or we could interpret it as avoidance or anger. If we interpret this person's reaction as the latter, how does that in turn affect our self-image and our future interactions with that individual? The way you answer this last question reveals whether or not you've embraced personal emotional responsibility.

As children, we need someone to provide comfort and affirmation. As we mature, however, we need to learn how to do this for ourselves as well. This typically starts to occur when a person reaches the point in development where he or she no longer blames external forces for the state of their life, or the entirety of their feelings. While it's recognized that no one exists in a vacuum and that externals certainly count for some of what we experience, this understanding is balanced with an acceptance of personal culpability.

The next developmental step, self-honesty, is hard for a lot of people. Here, the individual accepts their own feelings and begins to try to unravel their source, whether it's fear, excitement, worry, anger, zeal, or whatever. Now rather than simply give themselves over to the emotion, that feeling's considered more critically and truthfully, no hiding, no suppression, but an honest experience of feeling within the sacred self. As a result, this is typically when an individual finds one or two other people with whom they can share those real feelings in trustfulness. This sharing leads to emotional responsibility and openness.

There is a time and place for all things, including our feelings. Randomly venting any emotion can have great or terrible results. Yet, the willingness to be open outweighs the dangers of suppressing the true, sacred self. Eventually, the expression of these emotions will find the right venue in which to play themselves out freely, without guilt or regret. This also helps the individual internalize the lesson of that honestly expressed emotion. For example, repressed anger rarely heals; it just accumulates. If we instead speak the truth of our feelings, we then open the door to release the negative and build the positive. Making time for both feelings and healing is very important in the trust-love-will tripod. This doesn't mean being aggressive; it simply means respecting your own emotions as you would the emotions of any other sacred being. This is part of being God/dess.

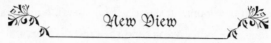

Are there areas in your life in which you feel you're being emotionally irresponsible? If so, what are they and why do you think you've allowed this situation to continue? What steps can you take to begin to be more emotionally responsible in all areas of your life, especially spiritually?

Head Versus Heart

We cannot consider emotional responsibility without also recognizing dependency. The Neo-Pagan worldview says that each individual is his or her own guru and guide, meaning each of us is personally responsible for our emotional health. Like perfect love and trust, this is a wonderful goal that's not always easily achieved.

Emotional reliance seeks to find a sense of self from externals. It manifests itself in a variety of ways including overeating, playing video games endlessly, overspending, and dramatizing the most mundane of things. Spiritually speaking, this person may surround himself with things that represent faith, but never truly manifest those beliefs in daily life. They are likely to be swayed by spiritual fads to feel more accepted. Let's put this into an example. Say a priest expresses disappointment with someone's efforts. The emotionally dependent individual feels rejection and believes that this negative feeling is all the priest's fault. There will be a lingering sense of shame, pain, and inadequacy that lead to overreacting, and extreme efforts to regain acceptance.

The emotionally responsible person, however, goes through a more thoughtful process. They might first wonder if the priest's disappointment is due to something else, like just having a bad day or the desire to show authority more strongly. Next, he or she considers if there is value to the observation, and if there is, takes actions to try and work things out. Typically, the first step is honest communication, even if that means agreeing to disagree. If that's not possible, then a time out may be called where both people take time to ponder their reactions, stabilize, then return to talk about things like mature adults.

This example illustrates why being able to balance our heads and hearts is so important not only to being emotionally responsible but also to nurturing the trust-love-will trinity. There needs to be a healthy, mutually-agreeable framework within which rationality and emotion dance (love and will). Sometimes, being selfish is a "good" thing and other times, it's just plain greed. Sometimes saying "no" is a "good" and incredibly loving thing, and sometimes it's just a way to avoid responsibility. The wisdom lies in recognizing the difference.

Commandment 10

The Judeo-Christian Tenth Commandment says, Thou shalt not covet thy neighbour's house, thou shalt not covet thy neighbour's wife, nor his manservant, nor his maidservant, nor his ox, nor his ass, nor any thing that is thy neighbour's.

Neo-Paganism instructs, For the greatest good an' it harm none.

The spiral of enlightenment moves ever onward and upward. Some Seekers follow along slowly, others steadily, and others still press and push to reach ever inward and upward. At first, the journey was focused on that initial step, the bold experiment in Be-ing. Next, the Seeker stretched a little further, rediscovering the Divine spark in Self and all things. As time moved on, these people began recognizing the basic checks and balances in the universe, and basic ethics with which to guide daily thought and action. For this great gift, Seekers are immensely grateful and further motivated to do what is good, noble, loving, true-to-vision, and truly sacred.

Closer and closer shines the light. The progressing soul sees a different picture through that illumination, guiding him or her toward touching the Monad and reuniting with that Power. And in that glorious "aha" moment we know ... these secrets, this path, was never hidden. Deity never disappeared. The patterns of all energy and of creation itself have always been with us, in us, and around us. It was simply a matter of remembering and reawakening that spiritual spark. Once ablaze, it becomes a beacon for thought and action, for the greatest good, an' it harm none—Fiat!

For the Greatest Good, an' It Harm None

*Y*ou know the old saying, "What you think is good for you often isn't?" That's true, no matter how wise or adept you become. And it's also true when we're talking globally about our greater tribes and communities. The goal of working for the greatest good—for the good of all—can easily become tainted by personal agendas, politics, and misinformation. How do we grow beyond those things and release both our lives and our magick from the rules imposed by years of societal pressures?

First, it's important to understand the concept of a common good, the theory that, somehow, there is an underlying drive in humankind, an empathy that seeks out the best for all people. This is most easily seen during times of disaster when waves of compassion come from all corners of the world, even from people who might otherwise seem stoic and detached. This feeling isn't vague; it's intimate, intense, and measurable on many levels.

We know that humans are social and tribal creatures. Our instinct is to be part of a group. We wish for the betterment of that group. True, this wish isn't wholly selfless, but it does create a common bond that considers the needs and goals of others rather than focusing solely on our own needs and goals. As our sense of the common good matures, there will naturally be times when another's needs, or a group's needs, outweigh our own. These are the moments in which the phrase "greatest good" begins to take on whole new meaning in our souls. Note, however, that sometimes the "greatest good" is also *your* good. One need not always be totally selfless in the quest for enlightenment. As we have seen throughout this book, the health and well-being of each person affects the larger picture (as within, so without).

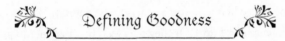

Defining Goodness

When you think about the word "good" what synonyms come immediately to mind? Make a list of words that mean "good" to you. Now consider each word. What people in your life come to mind who live those words? Which of those attributes would you like to develop in yourself? Are there any times when you can see positive actions as potentially having negative results?

For this greatest good to become a reality in the world, it must somehow begin manifesting economically, politically, philosophically, etc. Modern life makes this manifestation of good a very difficult and complex task. Not only do we have people in group A who think they know what this "good" should be (and are more than happy to impose that goodness any time the opportunity presents itself), but we also have plenty of individuals (group B) who are content with the status quo (the "if it's not broken, don't fix it" outlook).

Both groups have intrinsic issues to contend with. Group A often truly believes that what it desires is a noble thing. These people are driven by a value system that does not allow for any other reality because it might disturb their comfort zone. Humans want to be right. If we admit we could be wrong, we become vulnerable and those black and white lines we've used to guide our thoughts and actions suddenly become ours to draw. That means a lot of responsibility. So the core problem with group A is an unwillingness to think for themselves and take responsibility for those thoughts and actions. They assign blame or praise to whatever drives their values (such as God).

Group B suffers from apathy, lack of motivation, or a sense of being overwhelmed. These individuals may say, "I'm only one person, what can I do?" Or they may feel that it's easier to just try and avoid the potholes in the road, go with the flow, and hope for the best.

But we can see that just accepting the status quo isn't working. We have not really learned from history. We continue to repeat the same mistakes. Those potholes are growing larger no matter how hard we try to ignore them.

Then there's someone who belongs to neither group. This is the awakened soul who may also feel small when pondering the very large and often daunting significance of "the good of all." The "good of all" is certainly a grand ideal that would require tremendous changes in the majority of humankind to implement completely. So the seeker begins back at square one: with the sacred self.

Defining Ourselves

Defining ethics and morals is part of the process of becoming an established religion. As the Neo-Pagan movement grows and matures, we and our children struggle with ethical questions, especially since on the surface Neo-Paganism seems to advocate an "anything goes" outlook. Dig a little deeper, however, and you find a people of great conviction, many of whom are truly trying to "walk their talk." How we go about determining personal ethics in a sea of options? How do our personal ethics figure into the "greatest good, an' it harm none" paradigm?

We've talked about the goals of perfect love, perfect compassion, the quest for peace. All of these, if kept in balance, are noble and worthy of our energy. In fact, each awakened soul has a responsibility to strive for those goals personally, institutionally, socially, and in every way possible so that we become cocreators in human fulfillment. That's a pretty tall order, but "the good of all" doesn't leave a lot of wiggle room. The first real step is defining self in terms of these goals, both as individuals and part of that greater global community.

First, there are the roles to which we're born. We are someone's child. We may also be someone's brother or sister. It is true that we have no choice in how we're born, but how we interact with our setting and the other characters in our life's play is within our choosing. While both nature and nurture affect an individual's outlooks and behaviors, our strong independent streak can't be ruled out when we see where this initial role takes us.

Second, there are also the roles we've grown into. Here, we might become someone's spouse, employee, volunteer, student, teacher, leader, healer, etc. Each of us wears many hats in a lifetime, and in each of those roles we can find a way to create a little magick by moving beyond conventional thinking into something unique and remarkable. This mature spiritually actualized identity is one key to unlocking "the good of all." We cannot truly comprehend goodness globally until we find and activate it locally and within ourselves. (As within, so without).

To give a personal example, I'm a wife and a mother. I weave magick into my daily activities (like cooking) so that those people and things I most treasure are blessed by that energy. This is an example of activated, localized goodness. It's by no means perfect, but the goal of creating an at-home foundation that supports the "good of all" is in the forefront of my mind as I go through the day; the hope being that by living "goodness" I am also generating a greater good.

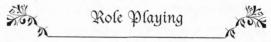

Role Playing

What roles do you play in your life? Make a list of your roles, then ponder them. Are there ways to bring magick and spiritual vision into the roles you play for localized goodness? How does each role affect the others? How do they combine in you when you focus on the intention of the "greatest good"?

Before going on, it's important to remind ourselves that understanding, actualizing, and embracing our roles isn't a once-in-a-lifetime deal. We can't just do it once and be done with it. Every moment of living changes us, and that means what was wholly good and right last year (or even an hour ago) may be wholly ridiculous or wrong right now. Let's take a childhood example. Say you loved the Old West when you were a child and had all kinds of cowboy stuff. As an adult, you have decided you're antigun. Does this mean you rid yourself of all those treasured memories and mementoes from your youth? Probably not. But you might hesitate to pass down your toy guns to your children or grandchildren. Your role has changed from that of a playful child to an informed adult who makes informed decisions guided by ethics.

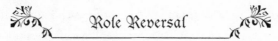

Role Reversal

After reading this example, can you think of times when one of the roles in your life puts you in an awkward ethical situation? How do these roles and situations make you feel today? Do you have options that could support the greatest good? If so, what are they? How do you realistically put those options in motion?

Time waits for none of us. Thus the moment to begin working toward goodness is now. To do this, we must be fully aware of the path we take to meet our goals.

Defining the Path

Know thyself. So much in this book comes back to knowing ourselves and being true to ourselves. In a vision-filled tradition the self is a nucleus or mandala of activity. Part of the process of becoming wholly aware and actualized is also moving from local to global perspectives of all that our lives touch; our choices, the outcomes from those choices, the paths we take for better or worse.

Let's consider our faith as having three potential paths.

Path One. The first path doesn't need a lot of definition. It's already well-marked, and you can simply go where it leads (enjoying the scenery along the way). Wicca is a good example where we have plenty of ground on which to build. Note, however, that this having markers and guidelines is not the same as adhering to strict dogma. The Wiccan seeker will pass the same landmarks, but for each individual, these images and symbols have special and specific meanings, even if some significance is universal. We will each understand the beauty of Wicca's landmarks uniquely in our own hearts, and we will each express the travelogue a little bit differently. We'll each, if you will, watch the pictures taken from masters and learn from them, but likely take very different pictures for our scrapbooks, even when we take them of the same landmarks and vistas.

When we walk with others along the Wiccan path, we'll point out to them what's worth looking at, explain why it's worth looking at. Even the well-worn paths are new and wondrous to all who walk them the first time. Additionally, those well-worn paths widen and narrow, and change their meanders, sometimes slightly, sometimes greatly, over time and in response to all the feet that walk them.

Path Two. The second path requires a little more effort. You might still be able to see the established pathways, but there are also some difficult landscapes to overcome. These paths aren't as populated, nor is the terrain as gentle to our feet. This path requires a more experienced hiker, one who is prepared for the inevitable twists and turns, rises and dips. One example of this path might be the Cabala (Jewish mysticism whose imagery is integrated into most Tarot decks), which is precise and studious in its approach to the journey. Now the seeker needs a good set of shoes and some equipment, not to mention a good guide, to reach his or her goal.

Path Three. The third path is one that opens by virtue of one person's footsteps alone. The Seeker may come to a clearing from time to time where there's a chance encounter with others that may share his experience, but for the most part walking the third path is a solitary adventure in which significant landmarks are significant only to the individual. This path is thus like a vision quest. Most often, it's the older souls who choose such a challenge. They become the walkers between the worlds: the shamans, the healers, the visionaries who see and live globally, but who are also often misunderstood.

Not everyone is meant to walk all three of these paths. Each path has a purpose and function, and each offers something different to the Seeker. Our task, therefore, is to determine which path will lead us to that priestly perspective, that greatest good, every moment of every day. Once we start down a path, we need to be aware that there are smaller paths to the left and right. There are times when we might want to walk in the middle of the path and times when we might want to get off the pavement and enjoy the grass beside the path.

Door Number 1, 2, or 3, or, What's in the Box

Which of the three archetypal paths do you feel you've chosen? Do you still feel this choice is best when pondering your personal good? The greatest good? Why or why not? If for some reason you're sensing that a new direction is necessary, which of the three paths will best help you achieve that goal?

Taking It Out of the Box

In Jungian psychology, an archetype is a universal or ideal pattern that is expressed in humankind's thoughts repeatedly. In applying this idea to paths, the way those patterns express themselves in thought and action become infinite in variety because of each person's uniqueness. In effect, the archetype's presence and significance cannot help but be changed by individual perception. Thus, it's important to recognize that these three basic paths are simply models to which each person brings something new and unique. We interact with and transform landscapes and the destination at the end can be likewise wholly unique. Don't get so caught up in structure that you forget the overall goal.

At some juncture we need to release our societal, cultural, familial, and personal boxes and build on heartfelt truths. Any thought, any action can become a limiting box. This box sometimes protects what's inside it and even makes that item more valuable (like a collectable doll). Here the box is part of a comfortable structure.

In other cases, however, we can't appreciate the contents of a box because we can't get close to it. Then too, what if it is *you* in the box—a stifling box, one that's hard to open—ones tied up tightly also offer an odd sense of security. Moving out from that environment is often scary, but that's also where the fresh air, the fresh idea, the fresh vision lies.

Having said that, not all conditioning is bad, nor is all independence good. We learn from our parents to be wary of fire because it can burn. That respect is a kind of experiential conditioning that has value to our long-term survival. Similarly, acting independently without information (touching the fire) can prove very painful. In effect, in getting out of our boxes perhaps the real question is whether we use our conditioning, or it uses us? Dependence and independence are symbiotic—we need a little of both to affect change wisely.

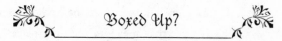

Boxed Up?

What do you perceive as boxes in your life? How do they obstruct your personal (local) and global goals of goodness? What boxes do you feel you still need? Why? What ones do you want to begin to take apart, or get out of altogether? Set some realistic goals and start unwrapping.

Don't just go jumping quickly out of a box without considering the possible results. Even as you would check a pool for water, there are some boxes you may need for a while, and some boxes are good for us (such as those we give our children to teach them what's safe). "An' it harm none" applies to yourself, as well.

The Good of All

The good of all people depends on having people who practice goodness, who teach goodness, who breath it and live it. The good of all depends on making that philosophy a tradition that we pass down from generation to generation. It must begin to live in the hearts and minds of all.

The scriptures of all world religions have asked their deities this question: *What would you have me do?* When we consider "as within, so without," we are also asking this of our own heart and soul. What sacred duties are we ready to accept? What attributes do we still need to develop before moving into tasks with greater responsibilities? How can each of us become part of the good of all?

Visualize this as a giant puzzle that the Seeker assembles piece by piece. Each piece that goes into the right place creates a little more light and begins to reveal the patterns of the Great Mystery. At first it's just a little flicker, but the Mystery urges the Seeker to keep trying to assemble that puzzle. Then the light grows brighter and attracts other individuals who want to help finish the picture, each bringing their own piece of the puzzle to add, each sharing their light. Neo-Paganism is a young religion. Many of us are still learning about interacting with other members of the community and with the world at large.

Writing this book has been an incredible learning process. I have found myself writing a little, walking away, thinking . . . pacing . . . yelling . . . laughing, and crying. As I struggled with each ethical question in my mind and heart, I sensed the labor pains that come with creating a coherent, functional religion. I've realized that what I'm feeling is something with which many of our elders and teachers have likewise struggled to bring up the next generation of spiritual seekers in the best manner possible.

I offer us all a challenge: Individuals: stop thinking of yourself in solitary terms. See yourself as a potential cornerstone that other people could turn to for strength, support, a sense of belonging. Groups: think of yourself as part of a virtual temple, built by one person at a time, one community at a time, in those moments when we each say, "We accept our power and our place" . . . "we accept that we can be greater" (or using Jesus' teachings: greater things shall you do).

Think of the present as a gateway to a better future. While we must "be here, now," the message of the greatest good must continue forward in time; it must maintain continuity or like an untended fire, it will go out. We need our practices and our structures, our passion and our logic, our stillness and our action to succeed. Each of us needs to be a scroll upon which the message of goodness is written, conveyed, and preserved for eternity. True happiness and fulfillment, both personally and globally, come from positive thoughts and acts, from being generous, kind, loving, and wise. All "good" things, for the Good of All. *Let it be.*

Bibliography

Adler, Margot. *Drawing Down the Moon*. Boston, MA: Beacon Press, 1979.

Aldington, Richard, translator. *New Larousse Encyclopedia of Mythology*. Middlesex, England: Hamlyn Publishing, 1973.

Ann, Marthaa, and Dorothy Myers Imel. *Goddesses in World Mythology*. New York, NY: Oxford University Press, 1995.

Arrien, Angeles, Ph.D. *The Four Fold Way*. New York, NY: Harper Collins, 1993.

Artress, Dr. Lauren. *Walking a Sacred Path*. New York, NY: Riverhead Books, 1995.

Bartlett, John. *Familiar Quotations*. Boston, MA: Little Brown & Co., 1938.

Black, William George. *Folk Medicine*. New York: Burt Franklin, 1883.

Bruce-Mitford. *Miranda Illustrated Book of Signs & Symbols*. New York, NY: DK Publishing, 1996.

Budge, E. A. Wallis. *Amulets & Superstitions*. Oxford, England: Oxford University Press, 1930.

Cavendish, Richard. *A History of Magic*. New York, NY: Taplinger Publishing, 1979.

Cooper, J. C. *Symbolic & Mythological Animals*. London, England: Aqarian Press, 1992.

Cunningham, Scott. *Crystal, Gem & Metal Magic*. St. Paul, MN: Llewellyn Publications, 1995.

———. *Encyclopedia of Magical Herbs*. St. Paul, MN: Llewellyn Publications, 1988.

Davison, Michael Worth, editor. *Everyday Life Through the Ages*. Pleasantville, NY: Reader's Digest Association Ltd., 1992.

Every Day Life through the Ages. London, England: Readers Digest Association, Berkley Square, 1992.

Fortune, Dion. *Psychic Self-Defense*. Boston, MA: Weiser, 1999.

Gordon, Leslie. *Green Magic*. New York, NY: Viking Press, 1977.

Gordon, Stuart. *Encyclopedia of Myths and Legends*. London, England: Headline Book Publishing, 1993.

Haggard, Howard W. MD. *Mystery, Magic and Medicine*. Garden City, NY: Doubleday & Co., 1933.

Hall, Manly P. *Secret Teachings of All Ages*. Los Angeles, CA: Philosophical Research Society, 1977.

Hutton, Ronald. *Triumph of the Moon*. Oxford, NY: Oxford University Press, 1999.

Jordan, Michael. *Encyclopedia of Gods*. New York, NY: Facts on File, Inc., 1993.

Kieckhefer, Richard. *Magic in the Middle Ages*. Melbourne Australia: Cambridge University Press, 1989.

Kunz, George Frederick. *Curious Lore of Precious Stones*. New York, NY: Dover Publications, 1971.

Leach, Maria, editor. *Standard Dictionary of Folklore, Mythology, and Legend*. New York, NY: Harper & Row, 1984.

Leach, Marjorie. *Guide to the Gods*. Santa Barbara, CA: ABC-Clio, 1992.

Lurker, Manfred. *Dictionary of Gods & Goddesses, Devils & Demons*. New York, NY: Routledge & Kegan Paul Ltd., 1995.

Magnall, Richmal. *Historical and Miscellanious Questions*. London, England: Longman, Brown, Green and Longman, 1850.

Metzger, Bruce, and Michael Coogan, editor. *The Oxford Companion to the Bible*. New York, NY: Oxford University Press, 1995.

Meyer, Marvin, and Richard Smith. *Ancient Christian Magic*. New York, NY: Harper SanFrancisco, 1994.

Murray, Keith. *Ancient Rites & Ceremonies*. Toronto, Canada: Tudor Press, 1980.

Paulsen, Kathryn. *The Complete Book of Magic & Witchcraft*. New York NY: Signet Books, 1970.

Russell, Jeffry R. *A History of Witchcraft.* New York, NY: Thames & Hudson, 1980.

Sjoo, Monica, and Barbara Mor. *The Great Cosmic Mother.* San-Francisco, CA: Harper & Row, 1987.

Spence, Lewis. *The Encyclopedia of the Occult.* London, England: Bracken Books, Studio Editions Ltd., 1994.

Telesco, Patricia. *How to Be a Wicked Witch.* New York, NY: Fireside, 2001.

Valiente, Doreen. *The Charge of the Goddess.* Brighton, England: Hexagon Publications, 2000.

Walker, Barbara. *The Woman's Dictionary of Symbols & Sacred Objects.* San Francisco, CA: Harper & Row, 1988.

Waring, Philippa. *The Dictionary of Omens & Superstitions.* Secaucus, NJ: Chartwell Books, 1978.

Wasserman, James. *Art and Symbols of the Occult.* Rochester, VT: Destiny Books, 1993.

Waterhawk, Don, and Patricia Telesco. *Sacred Beat.* Boston, MA: Red Wheel, 2003.

Websters Universal Unabridged Dictionary. New York, NY: World Syndicate Publishing, 1937.

Westwood, Jennifer. *Sacred Journies.* New York, NY: Henry Holt and Company, 1997.

Wilber, Ken. *The Holographic Paradigm and Other Paradoxes.* Boston, MA: Shambhala, 1988.

Index

ethics, 177
  of Neo-paganism, 211
  situational, 34–38, 143–44
evil, 31–32. *See also* "bad"
  witches; black magick

F

family, sacredness of, 138–42
financial service, 116–17
Five Pillars of Islam, xviii–xix
flawed gurus, 21–22
forgiveness, 199
Fortune, Dion, 171

G

Gaia, 48
giving, 89
God/dess
  connecting with, 8–17
  thou art, 1–5, 133–34
God-self, relationship with,
  17–22
good, common, 208–13, 218–19
goodness, 209
"good" witch, 173–76
gratitude, attitude of, 74–75,
  87–93
gray magick, 33
greater good, 208–13, 218–19
Great Rite, 152–59
gurus, flawed, 21–22

H

Hinduism, xiv–xv
holy places, 51
homosexuality, 151–52
honesty, xv
humility, xiv

I

inaction, 34–38, 176
individualism, 139–40

infatuation, 193
inner awareness, 44
instincts, 32
interconnectedness, 25–27
interpersonal relationships,
  148–49
invoking, 38, 42–43
Islam, xviii–xix

J

Jainism, xxi
Jesus Christ, x
journaling, 93
Judaism, xi–xii

K

Kali, 32
karma, 34–36, 164, 181

L

language, power of, 64–69
Law of Attraction, 179–81
Law of Return, 180, 181
Law of Three. *See* Threefold
  Law
leaders, 111–14
  effective, 111–12
  serving, 114–17
life
  examination of your, 18–21
  as reflection of beliefs, 75–79
  sacredness of all, 126–44
listening, 44, 66
living mindfully, 57–60
loosing, 38, 40–41
love, 186
  defined, 189–92
  emotional responsibility and,
    200–203
  forms of, 192–93
  imperfect, 194–96
  power of, 189